Report of the Working Group on the Management of Higher Education in the Maintained Sector

Presented to Parliament
by the Secretary of State for Education and Science
by Command of Her Majesty
March 1978

LONDON
HER MAJESTY'S STATIONERY OFFICE
£1·35 net

Cmnd 7130

The estimated cost of the preparation of this Report is £34,460 of which £1,760 represents the estimated cost of printing and publication.

March 1978

Dear Secretary of State,

On 7 February 1977 you announced the establishment of our Working Group with the following terms of reference:-

> 'To consider measures to improve the system of management and control of higher education in the maintained sector in England and Wales and its better coordination with higher education in the universities and, in the light of developments in relation to devolution and local authority finance, what regional and national machinery might be established for these purposes.'

I now have the honour of submitting our report which bears the unanimous endorsement of the Group as a whole.

Yours sincerely,

GORDON OAKES

The Right Honourable Shirley Williams MP
Secretary of State for Education and Science

Contents

Members of the Working Group

Mr G J Oakes MP
Minister of State for Education and Science

Sir Philip Rogers
Formerly Permanent Secretary, Department of Health and Social Security

Lord Alexander of Potterhill
Formerly Secretary, Association of Education Committees

Mr J V Barnett
Principal, The College of Ripon and York St John

Sir Ashley Bramall
Leader, Inner London Education Authority; Chairman, Council of Local Education Authorities

Mr S Broadbridge (from 1/9/77)
General Secretary, National Association of Teachers in Further and Higher Education

Mr K Brooksbank
Formerly Chief Education Officer, City of Birmingham

Mr W Y E Cairns (until 5/5/77)
Formerly Chairman, Nottinghamshire Education Committee

Mr F C A Cammaerts
Principal, Rolle College; President, National Association of Teachers in Further and Higher Education

Sir Michael Clapham
Formerly Chairman, Council for National Academic Awards

Mrs Elizabeth Coker
Essex County Council; Chairman, Association of County Councils Executive Council

Mr D Andrew Davies (from 6/5/77)
Secretary, Welsh Joint Education Committee

Mr T Driver (until 31/8/77)
Formerly General Secretary, National Association of Teachers in Further and Higher Education

Mr D B Edwards
Principal, Rotherham College of Technology; Member, National Executive, National Association of Teachers in Further and Higher Education

Mr L H Farnsworth
Principal, Brighton Technical College; Immediate Past President, Association of Principals of Colleges

Lord Heycock (until 5/5/77)
Formerly Chairman, Welsh Joint Education Committee

Mr J Horrell
Cambridgeshire County Council; Chairman, Association of County Councils Education Committee; Vice-Chairman, Council of Local Education Authorities

Cllr P Horton
Chairman, City of Sheffield Education Committee; Chairman, Association of Metropolitan Authorities Education Committee

Mr D E A Jones
Chief Executive, Gwynedd County Council

Dr H Kay
Vice-Chancellor, Exeter University

Mr P Knight
Secretary and Clerk to the Governors, Polytechnic of North London

Dr P Knight
Senior Lecturer, Plymouth Polytechnic; Vice-President, National Association of Teachers in Further and Higher Education

Mr T G Mercer
Managing Director, Thomas Mercer Ltd and Vice-Chairman, Governing Body of Hatfield Polytechnic

Dr R M W Rickett
Director, Middlesex Polytechnic

Mr J A Springett
County Education Officer, Essex County Council

Dr A Suddaby
Provost, City of London Polytechnic; Chairman, Committee of Directors of Polytechnics

Dr W Taylor
Director, University of London Institute of Education

Cllr M Thornton
Formerly Leader, Wirral Metropolitan Borough Council

Cllr M G Venn
Chairman, Standing Conference of Regional Advisory Councils for Further Education

Mr J P Carswell (Assessor) (until 31/12/77)
Formerly Secretary, University Grants Committee

Mr G F Cockerill (Assessor) (from 1/1/78)
Secretary, University Grants Committee

The following attended meetings of the Working Group or sub-groups as alternates:

Mr D T M Bennett
Joint Secretary, Standing Conference of Regional Advisory Councils for Further Education

Mr J S Bevan
Deputy Education Officer, Inner London Education Authority

Dr W Bosley
Principal, Slough College of Higher Education

Mr I G Cunningham
Education Officer, Association of County Councils

Mr J H Davies
Head of Further Education Department, Welsh Joint Education Committee

The late Mr B J Griffiths
Formerly Head of Further Education Department, Welsh Joint Education Committee

Professor N Haycocks
Academic Secretary, Universities Council for the Education of Teachers

Mr C C Jasper
County Treasurer, Hertfordshire County Council

Dr E Kerr
Chief Officer, Council for National Academic Awards

Mr E St J Moss
Under-Secretary, University Grants Committee

Mr W J Richardson
Head of Department, Polytechnic of Central London; Member, National Executive, National Association of Teachers in Further and Higher Education

Mr P T Sloman
Education Officer, Association of Metropolitan Authorities

Mr J Taylor
Associate Director, Bristol Polytechnic

Secretariat:

Mr M J G Smith
Department of Education and Science

Mr K Robinson (until 31/1/78)
Department of Education and Science

CHAPTER I

Introduction

1.1. Our membership and terms of reference were announced by the Secretary of State for Education and Science on 7 February 1977. Our membership is given at the front of this report; our terms of reference were as follows:

'To consider measures to improve the system of management and control of higher education in the maintained sector in England and Wales and its better coordination with higher education in the universities and, in the light of developments in relation to devolution and local authority finance, what regional and national machinery might be established for these purposes.'

1.2. We met for the first time on 16 February 1977 and over the past twelve months have had a further 10 meetings. In addition, two sub-groups have each had five meetings.

1.3. At the outset we agreed that we ought to produce a report as quickly as the complexity of the subject permitted. To facilitate this we agreed that members could, where necessary, be represented by alternates at meetings which they could not themselves attend. The persons who attended meetings of the full Group or of sub-groups are also listed at the front of our report and we should like to extend to them our thanks for their contribution to the work of the Group.

1.4. We did not issue a general invitation to submit evidence. We are however grateful to the 20 organisations and individuals listed at Appendix A who submitted written evidence; we have given it careful consideration and it has contributed materially to our conclusions.

1.5. At our first meeting we decided that our deliberations should be confidential. In the event certain items have appeared in the press purporting to reflect our views on individual items. We hope that readers of our report will now consider it as a whole and pay particular attention to the overall context in which we have framed our recommendations.

CHAPTER II

Development and Organisation of the Public Sector of Higher Education

Historical Background

2.1. The development of higher education outside the universities has its roots in the nineteenth century and from an early stage there was a local authority involvement. Already by the first half of the 1880s Liverpool Corporation and Nottingham Town Council had contributed to the establishment of colleges in their towns, and under legislation in 1889 and 1890 councils were empowered to levy a penny rate and to divert for purposes of technical education funds originally intended as compensation for publicans deprived of their licences; in the period 1890–1902 these and other funds were used for the construction of 12 polytechnics and technical institutions in London and of 13 in the provinces.

2.2 The establishment of local education authorities (LEAs) in 1902 with powers to provide education beyond the elementary stage led to further development, including the setting up of the first municipal teacher training colleges, and this received recognition in 1918 when local authorities' expenditure on post-elementary education became eligible for 50 per cent central government grant. Growth continued to be slow, however, with the main emphasis, except for teacher training, on part-time evening courses; by 1938/39 there were fewer than 6,000 full-time students following courses of higher education, other than teacher training, outside the universities.

2.3. The main stimulus to the growth of the system as we know it today came with the passing of the Education Act 1944 which required LEAs to prepare plans for further education in their areas. The 1956 White Paper on Technical Education[1] proposed a substantial increase in the output of advanced courses and introduced a four-tier system of Colleges of Advanced Technology (CATs), regional colleges, area colleges and local colleges. The CATs were intended to facilitate the development of advanced technology courses; in 1952 the Government had introduced a special 75 per cent rate of grant for such courses and this continued until 1959 when General Grant was introduced (paragraph 2.12). In 1961 the nine maintained CATs transferred from the local authority sector to become direct grant institutions, and following a recommendation of the Robbins Report on Higher Education[2] were granted university status; they now come under the aegis of the University Grants Committee.

2.4. The designation of the CATs and their eventual progression to university status left a number of regional colleges in the maintained sector with

---

[1]Technical Education Cmd. 9703.

[2]Report of the Committee on Higher Education under the Chairmanship of Lord Robbins (1963) Cmnd. 2154.

a substantial involvement in advanced work. The 1956 White Paper had listed 16 colleges, in addition to those eventually designated CATs, which were in receipt of the special advanced technology grant, and by 1962/63 two-thirds of the full-time students at the 25 regional colleges were engaged on work of an advanced character. A further White Paper in 1966[1] considered the future of these colleges and, emphasising the importance of a continuing significant local authority stake in higher education, proposed the formation from them of 28 Polytechnics (later increased to 30) to provide the focus for the development of a distinctive public sector, complementing the universities within a binary system of higher education. This policy, supplemented by the proposals of the 1972 White Paper[2] for the integration of teacher training with the rest of higher education (see paragraph 2.6 below), created the present structure of maintained higher education.

Growth and Extent of the Public Sector

2.5. The growth of the public sector of higher education over the last twenty years can be seen from the following table, which also gives planning figures for 1981/82 recently announced by the Department (November 1977):

Table 1: Full-time and Sandwich Students in Public Sector Higher Education (England and Wales)

	1954/55	1962/63	1969/70	1974/75	1976/77 (provisional)	1981/82 (planning)
Higher education (other than Teacher Training)	9,700[a]	38,300[a]	81,000	102,000	130,300	181,000
Teacher Training	24,300	47,700	109,200	108,200	85,300	38,000
Total Public Sector	34,000[a]	86,000[a]	190,200	210,200	215,600	219,000

[a]Including students in CATs

The same period saw an increase in part-time attendance with the number of day and evening students on courses of higher education (other than teacher training) growing from 100,000 in 1962/63 to almost 125,000 in 1976/77.

2.6. In accordance with the policy announced in the 1972 White Paper[2], the colleges of education (as teacher training colleges have been known since the middle 1960s) are currently being integrated with the rest of the higher education system, some by amalgamation with universities, polytechnics and other existing colleges and some by reorganisation as free-standing higher education institutions. The outcome, after closure of a number of colleges, will be a substantial reduction in the present number of institutions involved in higher education; in 1981 there will be around 400 public sector institu-

---

[1]A Plan for Polytechnics and Other Colleges: Higher Education in the Further Education System Cmnd. 3006.
[2]Education: A Framework for Expansion Cmnd. 5174.

tions with students on higher education courses, of which more than 200 will provide courses for full-time and sandwich students (for details see Table at Appendix B).

Public Sector Institutions

2.7. Most public sector higher education is provided in maintained institutions, ie in institutions owned and financed by LEAs. A significant contribution is, however, made by a number of colleges which operate under the aegis of charitable trusts and limited companies but which receive grant for up to 100 per cent of their capital and running costs. Included in the figures quoted in paragraph 2.6 are about 40 such colleges, comprising former voluntary colleges of education and direct grant further education institutions grant-aided by the Department of Eduction and Science (DES); mixed institutions (formed by amalgamation of former voluntary and maintained colleges) jointly grant-aided by DES and local education authorities; and establishments assisted by LEAs. The last of these three groups – of which the most notable examples are the five Inner London Polytechnics assisted by the Inner London Education Authority (ILEA) – are in the remainder of this report regarded as falling within the maintained sector.

Cost of the Public Sector

2.8. The net running cost of the maintained sector of higher education in 1976/77 at November 1976 prices was £394m of which polytechnics accounted for about £227m and other advanced work about £167m. (These figures include debt charges and are net of all income, including fee income – see paragraph 2.18 below – but do not include the cost of student maintenance awards.) The underlying estimated unit costs (cost per student) and student/staff ratios (SSRs) are given in the following table:

Table 2: Net Unit Costs and Student/Staff Ratios 1976/77 (England and Wales)[a]

	Overall		Laboratory-based[b]		Other	
	Unit Cost £	SSR	Unit Cost £	SSR	Unit Cost £	SSR
Polytechnics	2,000	8·1	2,250	7·0	1,650	9·3
Other advanced FE	1,400	8·9	1,580	7·7	1,150	9·8

[a]Source: DES (Unit Costs) and Pooling Committee (SSRs)
[b]Includes Art and Design

In addition there was recurrent expenditure from public funds of about £46m in 1976/77 (at November 1976 prices) in respect of the voluntary colleges of education.

2.9. The averages in Table 2 reflect differences in the range of work undertaken by the two categories of institution, with polytechnics in general offering the widest and most advanced range of courses. They also conceal a range of variations between institutions. For example, the cost per student in polytechnics ranged from £1,800 to £3,000 for laboratory-based students and from £1,350 to £2,250 for other students.

Salaries of Academic Staff

2.10. Over 60 per cent of the cost of higher education in the public sector is accounted for by salaries. Academic salaries are determined nationally (and have been since 1919) by negotiation within the Burnham further education committee. In addition to recommending salary scales for different categories of teacher, which are then given statutory effect by order of the Secretary of State under the terms of the Remuneration of Teachers Act 1965, the committee also makes recommendations about the distribution of posts on various scales in relation to the level of work undertaken.

Administration of Colleges

2.11. Local education authorities own the premises of maintained institutions and staff employed in them are appointed to their service; they have overall responsibility for the institutions' management, though they are required under the Education Act (No. 2) 1968 to establish governing bodies and academic boards whose functions are prescribed by articles of government for each institution. Similar arrangements apply to colleges in receipt of grant from DES and the Secretary of State is empowered under the Further Education Regulations 1975[1] to require them to be conducted in accordance with schemes of government agreed by her.

Pooling

2.12. The cost of maintained higher education has been shared among all LEAs since 1959. At that time, the previous system of percentage grants for various forms of education was replaced by General Grant in support of local authority services as a whole. In order to protect authorities with institutions engaged in higher education from having to bear a disproportionate financial burden and to safeguard the continued expansion of advanced technology courses which had previously attracted a special rate of grant (paragraph 2.3) the Government introduced a system of pooling the cost of advanced further education.

2.13. This is essentially the system in operation today, although since 1975 the further education pool has been merged with the previously separate teacher training pool, which had been in existence since 1945 (and in embryo since 1926). Under it, each LEA is assessed for a contribution to the pool on the basis of its school population and non-domestic rateable value and, in turn, is entitled without limitation to charge to the pool its expenditure on approved courses of higher education. Under Schedule 2 to the Local Government Act 1974 payment of net contributions to and receipts from the

---

[1] The Further Education Regulations 1975 SI No. 1054.

pool is made by adjusting the needs element of Rate Support Grant paid to each authority and the operation of the system as a whole is kept under review by a Pooling Committee which makes recommendations to the local authority associations and to the Secretary of State.

Courses—Approval and Validation

2.14. Until 1957 the Secretary of State's approval was required for the provision of all further education courses and was an important element in the control of expenditure on which grant was payable. In that year it was discontinued for non-advanced courses but retained for advanced courses on the grounds that they tended to require expensive staff and equipment.

2.15. Currently, each institution is responsible in conjunction with its maintaining authority for drawing up its academic development plan and for preparing individual course proposals. Advanced course proposals (except those for teacher training courses) are submitted for approval through the appropriate Regional Advisory Council (see Chapter IX). In certain cases the Council can grant approval on behalf of the Secretary of State, in others decisions are given by Regional Staff Inspectors (members of Her Majesty's Inspectorate) acting on her behalf after advice from the Regional Advisory Council.

2.16. Some institutions run courses (including some at post-degree level) leading to their own diplomas. Save for one or two specialised cases, however, institutions do not grant their own degrees and students are awarded those of the Council for National Academic Awards (CNAA) or universities. Degree courses require the academic approval (validation) of these bodies. Similar arangements exist for some non-degree courses and courses leading to qualifications of professional bodies. As a condition of validation certain requirements may be laid down in relation, for example, to libraries or staffing which have financial and management consequences.

Student Awards

2.17. Subject to certain residence and other requirements laid down nationally, higher education students are eligible for mandatory awards if they attend courses specified in the Awards Regulations.[1] Most full-time and sandwich courses are covered in this way, including first degree, initial teacher training, HND/HTD and DipHE courses. The grant is paid by the LEA in whose area the student is normally resident at rates prescribed in the Regulations, and comprises two elements: a payment for maintenance and a sum to cover the fees charged by the institution attended. In calculating the individual grant, account is taken of parental (or spouse's) income, if any. Ninety per cent of LEA expenditure on mandatory awards is reimbursed by the Government. (Students not eligible for mandatory awards may be given an award at the discretion of their LEA.)

---

[1]The Local Education Authorities Awards Regulations 1977 SI No. 1307.

Fees

2.18. For a number of years prior to 1977/78 fees charged for higher education courses represented less than 10 per cent of full costs (the figures quoted in paragraphs 2.8 and 2.9 take account only of fees at this lower level). For 1977/78 the Secretary of State recommended significantly higher levels of fees to be charged for advanced courses, raising fee income to about a fifth of total cost and correspondingly reducing the net cost of provision chargeable to the pool.

Setting-up of the Working Group

2.19. The arrangements for controlling and financing higher education in the maintained sector, as described above, have served well in a period of rapid growth. They do not, however, constitute an entirely satisfactory system of management and financial control and at a time when the cost of the maintained sector alone has risen to an estimated £396m (in 1978/79) their deficiencies and the need for improved mechanisms for planning and controlling expenditure have become increasingly clear. This has been recognised for some time and the local authorities have had discussions on the subject with the Department, both within and outside the Pooling Committee, over a number of years.

2.20. The 1972 White Paper[1] also endorsed the need for improved coordination of higher education in the public sector in order to facilitate its expansion and integration with teacher education. In the period following its publication discussions between the Department and representatives of the local authority associations were resumed. However, partly as a result of pressure arising from the reorganisation of local government and partly as a result of the decision to set up the Layfield Committee of Enquiry on Local Government Finance, it proved impossible to make progress at the time.

2.21. In 1975 the Council of Local Education Authorities (CLEA), representing both the Association of County Councils and the Association of Metropolitan Authorities, submitted to the Department proposals for a system of further education advisory councils in the regions and these formed the basis of widespread consultations in the autumn of that year. In the light of views then expressed it became clear to the Department that a comprehensive review was required of existing arrangements for the management of higher education in the maintained sector. Accordingly, in July 1976 the then Secretary of State, Mr Mulley, announced his intention to set up a Working Group to undertake such a review. We were appointed by the end of the year and started work in February 1977.

---

[1] Cmnd. 5174.

CHAPTER III

Our Terms of Reference: Some Underlying Assumptions

3.1. We were charged with the important practical task of considering how the management and control of higher education in the maintained sector could be improved and better coordinated with university higher education. Some evidence we received and some public comment have implied rather wider responsibilities. We wish, therefore, to set out some of the assumptions implicit in our terms of reference.

3.2. We accepted that

(a) local education authorities will be major providers of higher education, and this has ruled out of consideration the wholesale transfer of institutions to other management. We recognised, however, that some would advocate measures of this sort and failure on our part to recommend changes which commanded substantial public support could pave the way for such developments.

(b) while we were not bidden to consider non-advanced further education, our discussions should take cognisance of the close links between it and advanced further education.

(c) since our concern was with the maintained sector and its coordination with the universities, the role of the University Grants Committee in relation to the universities would be unchanged. Our recommendations for improved coordination with university provision are on this basis.

(d) the student awards system will continue broadly on present lines and in real terms fees will continue to make a significant contribution to the financing of higher education.

(e) there will continue to be a significant provision of higher education in institutions grant-aided by DES (paragraph 2.7).

(f) validation of courses and academic standards in maintained and direct grant institutions will continue in the hands of the CNAA, validating universities, the Business and Technician Education Councils and various professional bodies. We recognise, however, that the improved management of higher education cannot be divorced from questions of academic quality. We return to this question later.

3.3 We were required to have regard to developments in relation to devolution and local authority finance. On the former our recommendations for Wales (Chapter XI) take into account legislation now before Parliament; for England they assume that there will not be for some time to come, if ever, regional assemblies with powers and funds to play an executive regional role in managing higher education. The consultations on local authority finance since the Layfield Committee reported do not indicate any changes which might affect our report.

3.4. We have not attempted to form a considered view of the prospects for the development of higher education to which our recommendations might apply. However, births reached their peak in 1964 and have since declined by a third. The numbers of young persons in the age group 18 to 22 will reach a plateau in the period 1982–86 and thereafter decline gradually at first but more rapidly towards the end of the century. To avoid a decline in numbers from the 1982–86 level would require by the mid 1990s an increase of 50 per cent in the proportion of the age-group following higher education or far-reaching changes in the composition of the student body and in the needs which higher education has hitherto sought to meet.

3.5. While it would be unwise to make any precise assumptions about the trend of higher education numbers so far ahead, it is clear that the era of rapid expansion is coming to a close, and may be succeeded by a decline. On the other hand the relative demand for different types of education could continue to change at least as rapidly and unpredictably as in the past. To cope with such changes in a system which is no longer expanding rapidly will pose difficult management problems and demand a high level of adaptability.

3.6. The demographic pattern also has consequences for the structure of the system. Current capital programmes have been reduced by financial constraints. Major càpital programmes to expand capacity, which would only just come into use when numbers were in prospect of levelling-off, might be difficult to justify. Provision will be needed to adapt premises for other uses, but our recommendations should be compatible with the likelihood that until the mid 1980s provision will largely be based on the existing capacity in a wide variety of institutions, many of which will also be concerned with further education at non-advanced level.

CHAPTER IV

Objective, Functions and Criteria

4.1. In this chapter of our report we discuss the objective to which our recommendations should be directed, the functions we saw as necessary to the attainment of that objective, and the criteria on which we judge the possible effectiveness of various alternatives.

Objective

4.2. We have taken as our objective the creation of a management system which would make most effective use of the available resources to meet demand from students who qualify for higher education and, in so far as they can be assessed, future needs for qualified manpower.

4.3. We would emphasise the importance we attach to educational quality in relation to assessment of cost-effectiveness. We do not necessarily equate the latter with low unit costs and we see no reason to suppose that high unit costs are synonymous with quality; we believe that in many instances they are due to failure in the admittedly difficult task of matching supply to demand.

4.4 We have already recorded our assumption that existing bodies continue to be responsible for validation and safeguarding of academic standards. Attainment of the above objective will, however, require that the system of management we recommend should be equipped to make judgements of an academic character. This will require that the various bodies we envisage should have academics amongst their membership and ready access to expert professional advice.

4.5. Student demand and future needs for highly qualified manpower are, of course, met by higher education as a whole. Our objective will require coordination of the maintained sector with the universities and this is recognised in our terms of reference. The same applies to direct grant institutions and also to Welsh higher education in so far as our recommendations may, as a result of devolution, be inapplicable to Wales (see Chapter XI).

Functions

4.6. We identify four main categories of function to be performed by a management system:

(a) intelligence: the collection, analysis and dissemination of information relating to the demand for and supply of higher education;

(b) planning changes and developments which may be necessary to meet the demand foreseen;

(c) within limits set by the government, determining the necessary provision and where it should be made, and allocating resources accordingly; and

10

(d) oversight of the implementation of agreed plans and the cost-effectiveness of the system as a whole.

Functions (a) and (b) above will need to be carried out in close cooperation with the Department and the University Grants Committee. Functions (c) and (d), however, provided the plans are adequately coordinated with similar proposals for the universities, will be a matter solely for the arrangements we recommend later in this report.

Criteria

4.7. Although we reached a large measure of agreement in drawing up criteria which should guide us in our discussions some members would attach greater importance to some of the criteria discussed below than to others.

4.8. We would not regard the removal of all significant powers from individual maintaining authorities and their relegation to the position of agents of a national management system as compatible with the continuance of a maintained system of higher education. It has therefore been crucial to our discussion that we should formulate proposals which would lead to a fruitful partnership between individual local authorities and the centre, in which each had clearly defined responsibilities.

4.9. We are agreed that whatever defects there may be in the present arrangements for providing maintained higher education, the system has demonstrated remarkable resilience, adaptability, capacity for growth and ability to raise its academic standards. In comparing alternative proposals we have therefore preferred to proceed by evolution rather than revolution and, where possible, to build on what exists rather than propose quite new arrangements. Moreover, our recommendations for a national system of management and financial control have been deliberately framed to permit flexibility in the timetable for introducing the more radical of the changes which we propose.

4.10. The report of the Layfield Committee[1] criticised the present arrangements for the finance of maintained higher education for their lack of accountability. Throughout our considerations we have been concerned with this criterion and with other related concepts, and we have endeavoured to frame our recommendations with the following considerations in mind:

(a) those responsible for management decisions should be responsible, in part at least, for finding the funds to implement them and should be accountable (ultimately to the electorate) for both;

(b) the power to take decisions and the accompanying financial responsibility should, whever possible, be delegated downwards;

(c) powers and responsibilities at each level should be clearly understood and overlap of responsibilities avoided.

---

[1] Report of the Committee of Enquiry on Local Government Finance Cmnd. 6453.

The higher education system must inevitably be managed at a variety of levels, each of which should have appropriate functions and powers; some of these may be laid down by statute. Our recommendations are designed to minimise the contradictions inherent in this by clarifying responsibilities in such a way that individual authorities are accountable to their rate payers for the good administration of their institutions, and that Government, in partnership with local authorities, is accountable to the tax payer for the effectiveness of the system as a whole.

4.11. A significant minority of the evidence tendered to us, in effect, urged that management decisions should be left to local authorities and their governing bodies under a system of relative freedom with a minimum of national control. We have some sympathy with this approach but have felt bound to conclude that free competition in a public service like higher education, in which regional and national considerations play an important part, would not be effective. Nevertheless, our recommendations are designed to leave a significant area free for local initiative and recognise that an element of competition within guidelines laid down nationally is likely to be healthy in this respect. Although we emphasise later the need for adequate central machinery, we are anxious that an over-elaborate bureaucracy should not be created and believe that no national system can afford to neglect the additional flexibility and effectiveness which will result from leaving ample scope for local initiative.

4.12. Our recommendations must apply to higher education provided in a variety of institutions ranging widely in size and in the degree of their involvement in higher as opposed to further education. We do not believe, however, that the arrangements for controlling higher education in major institutions, such as polytechnics, can or should be the same as those applicable to a few advanced courses in a general-purpose further education establishment. We have therefore been at pains within a general framework to recommend different arrangements to meet different circumstances. Such arrangements we believe should not assign institutions to rigid categories which do not permit their transfer, by agreement with their maintaining authorities, from one arrangement to another. Equally, the different styles of management proposed should preserve reasonable equity between the authorities and institutions to which they are applied.

4.13. What is said in the immediately preceding paragraphs relates mainly to the decision-making process in management. We have not so far referred to the question of financial control, which is, of course, of equally fundamental importance and central to our terms of reference. We believe, however, that financial systems should be the servant and not the master of management. We have concentrated, in the first instance, therefore on designing a decision-making system which is rational and capable of achieving the objective outlined above; our recommendations on finance have been formulated to be compatible with our recommendations for management. While we believe that the former are sound in themselves, we would emphasise the importance of viewing them—and any alternatives—in the broader context outlined above.

CHAPTER V

A National System of Management and Control

5.1. In the previous chapter we identified four main functions which a management system would need to perform:

(a) intelligence: the collection, analysis and dissemination of information relating to the demand for and supply of higher education;

(b) planning changes and developments which may be necessary to meet the demand foreseen;

(c) within limits set by the Government, determining the necessary provision and where it should be made, and allocating resources accordingly; and

(d) oversight of the implementation of agreed plans and of the cost-effectiveness of the system as a whole.

A National Body

5.2. To exercise these functions as they affect the maintained sector of higher education we recommend the establishment of a new National Body with terms of reference on the following lines:

'To collect, analyse and present, where appropriate in conjunction with the Department of Education and Science and the University Grants Committee, information affecting the demand for and supply of higher education in the maintained sector; to advise the Secretary of State and the local authority associations on the total provision which should be made for it; to consider and issue guidance on the programmes and estimates submitted to it by authorities and, where appropriate, institutions; to allocate funds for recurrent expenditure and to advise on the allocation of capital expenditure; and to have general oversight of the development of maintained higher education and its cost-effectiveness.'

5.3. We think that the National Body should also have a role in relation to the direct grant and voluntary colleges which at present receive grant from the Department of Education and Science. We have not been able to consider this in detail since we were not properly constituted to do so, but we recommend that the providing bodies be invited to consider the possibility that the remit of the National Body might be extended at least to include responsibility for advising the Secretary of State on the plans of their colleges and on their financial support. Such a development would be particularly helpful in relation to the small group of new voluntary institutions (formed by mergers of former voluntary colleges of education and maintained colleges) which receive finance both from the Department and from a local education authority.

13

5.4. The National Body would represent a partnership of national and local interests reflecting the shared responsibility between national and local levels for management decisions within the system. In the rest of this chapter we examine the system of management and financial control which we recommend it should operate. We return in the next chapter to consider its membership.

Information

5.5. Experience since the Robbins Report[1] has shown how quickly the demand for higher education and its direction can change. In total the numbers of those willing and qualified to follow courses of higher education grew more rapidly until the early 1970s than the Robbins Committee expected. Thereafter, the rate of growth fell and is only now showing signs of revival. By sectors, the changes have been more marked; provision for teacher education which, in response to the needs of the schools, expanded almost threefold is now scheduled to revert to the levels of the early 1960s. The rapid growth in take-up of science and technology places was followed by a decline which has only recently shown signs of being reversed, while the subsequent growth in demand for academic social studies was in turn succeeded by a trend towards the professional disciplines of law and accountancy.

5.6. It fell, in particular, to the maintained sector to satisfy the marginal demand resulting from these changes; in doing so, it pressed into use local authority premises redundant for other purposes and leased or purchased accommodation from outside. As a result the total demand for higher education appeared to be reasonably satisfied at all times but at the cost of considerable overcrowding in some disciplines and quite unviable courses in others. To some degree this latter over-provision could be tolerated in an era when continued expansion could be confidently foreseen and places surplus to current requirements might be expected to be needed in a few years' time; by the mid 1980s, however, demand will, at best, be about static and the matching of supply to demand will be a much more difficult process requiring better information than is now available.

5.7. At national level the need is for information which will enable national demand for different types of courses, mainly at or above first degree level, to be matched with national supply. This will need a cooperative effort between, on the one hand, the Department of Education and Science and, on the other, the University Grants Committee and the new National Body, and they will need to make appropriate arrangements for the purpose. Provision of less-advanced courses, particularly in the field of business and technical studies, is largely confined to the maintained sector and is designed in the main to meet local needs, and the ascertainment of demand will in general fall to local authorities and their institutions, where necessary cooperating on a regional basis.

---

[1]Cmnd. 2154.

5.8. We should perhaps emphasise that we do not advocate the establishment of a major new statistical apparatus. The Department of Education and Science should remain responsible for the main collection of the basic data which the National Body will require; much of it is already available. We identify the following main needs:

(a) effort should be devoted to the analysis and interpretation of information already available, eg of trends in studies at O and A level in schools, which may affect demand for higher education.

(b) a deliberate policy of devoting statistical effort to operational purposes with greater weight attached to timeliness; information, for example, about the current supply/demand position in November/December would be valuable in making decisions for the next academic year while information in the following spring, even if more precise, is too late to be usable.

(c) closer study of the developments in the manpower field; although manpower studies are in most sectors still far from being a reliable guide to future demand for higher education it may be expected that their usefulness will increase, and experience shows that particular developments, eg in relation to accountancy and law, can have rapid repercussions on higher education.

(d) prompt and regular dissemination of available information; because the planning process operates at all levels from individual institutions to central government we attach particular importance to the best and most up-to-date information being widely available.

(e) further enquiry into the methodology of forecasting demand.

Capital Expenditure (Buildings and Equipment)

5.9. The National Body would have a role in relation both to capital and to recurrent expenditure. Capital expenditure on higher education is, by comparison, a small element in the total and will continue to be so in an era which is unlikely to see a rapid expansion of the system. The methods of controlling local authority capital expenditure are now under consideration with the local authority associations following publication of the Government's Green Paper on Local Government Finance[1]. Subject to this, however, we would envisage that the National Body would advise the Secretary of State both on the total share which should be devoted to higher education capital expenditure and how the agreed provision should be allocated to individual institutions.

Possible Financial Arrangements

5.10. On recurrent expenditure the terms of reference we have suggested above would assign to the National Body the strategic role of advising on the

---

[1]Cmnd. 6813.

total provision, determining in consultation with individual authorities the scale and nature of the provision in their institutions and the allocation of nationally provided funds accordingly. LEAs and their governing bodies would be responsible for the efficient and cost-effective management of their institutions in accordance with their agreed roles.

5.11. We take the view that this partnership in the decision-making process should be complemented and reinforced by a system of joint finance in which part of the cost is met nationally and part by individual maintaining authorities. At present, the whole cost is met nationally, ie shared amongst all authorities by a pooling mechanism, in recognition of the fact that the bulk of the provision is to meet national or regional rather than local needs and that equity demands that the cost should not fall on individual authorities who happen by historical accident to maintain the institutions concerned. We agree with the Layfield Committee that this arrangement is wrong in principle: first, because no overall limitation is placed on the total amount chargeable to the pool, and secondly, because local authorities should not be responsible for the disbursement of funds of which only an insignificant proportion falls to be borne by the ratepayers to whom they are accountable.

5.12. We have considered four possible alternatives:

(a) continuance of the present system of pooling, superimposing on it the National Body with the general role indicated above but without any powers to allocate financial resources;

(b) abandonment of pooling in favour of a recoupment system under which maintaining authorities could recoup from other authorities the cost of providing higher education for their students;

(c) a system under which the major part of the cost would be pooled and met from a fixed sum determined annually, which would be allocated between individual authorities or institutions by the National Body, and a minor part would be met direct by the maintaining authority itself;

(d) a system identical to (c) save that the National Body's funds would be made available not through a pooling mechanism but by direct grant from the Exchequer.

5.13. We quickly came to the conclusion that alternative (a) would be inadequate to meet the situation. It satisfies few of the criteria which we have adopted, would leave total expenditure an open-ended commitment and the National Body with no powers to secure the implementation of its decisions.

5.14. Abandonment of pooling in favour of recoupment was urged by some of the organisations and individuals who submitted evidence to us; a number of our members were also interested in it and we have examined the possibility carefully. At first sight, recoupment seems attractive in that it offers the possibility of exposing the higher education system to financial disciplines akin to those of the open market, and of placing the burden of cost on authorities to the extent that their students take advantage of the higher education provided. On closer examination these potential benefits are largely illusory and the offsetting disadvantages appear over-riding.

5.15. In principle, recoupment could be based on standard charges for various types of courses or on actual costs. In the former case, the wide variations of current costs would leave the maintaining authorities of higher cost institutions to meet a very large proportion of the total cost, in some cases nearly 50 per cent, from local revenues. The system would closely resemble one in which costs up to fixed amounts for each student depending on the type of course were poolable without the pooling system's advantage of being able to vary the incidence of cost between authorities as might appear from time to time equitable.

5.16. On the other hand, a system of recoupment based on actual costs would exercise no financial discipline on the maintaining authorities unless other authorities were able to refuse to authorise their students to attend courses whose costs they considered unreasonably high. This would conflict with the free choice which students have under present arrangements and which also underlies the mandatory awards system; as noted in paragraph 3.2(d) above, the latter is outside our terms of reference.

5.17. Recoupment on either basis would place an additional burden on the parent authority of a student attending a course in a maintained institution as opposed to a university and could lead to guidance on future study being biassed by extraneous financial considerations. Courses which only qualified for discretionary awards would also be at great risk.

5.18. The maintaining authority would be left with the financial risk of courses failing to recruit adequately, while the National Body would have no financial resources to encourage courses which appeared to be in the national interest. Our members' experience of difficulties over recoupment in relation to non-advanced courses makes us dubious of claims that the administration of a recoupment system would not be cumbersome and a cause of much dispute about individual students. Finally, it would still be necessary to make some provision akin to pooling for overseas and other students for whom no individual authority could be held responsible.

5.19. We have felt bound to conclude that the introduction of recoupment as a financial basis for maintained higher education would be administratively complicated and inflexible and debilitating to the health of the system as a whole.

5.20. Alternatives (c) and (d) have much in common and can conveniently be considered together. Under each the major element of finance would be provided from central funds under the control of the National Body within a total to be determined annually. Similarly, each would provide for individual maintaining authorities to have a significant financial stake in the institutions they maintain, and in so far as individual institutions were concerned the two systems would appear virtually identical.

5.21. The source of funds has implications for the constitution of the National Body. If they were provided by direct grant the National Body would be accountable to Parliament through the Secretary of State with the corollary that its membership would need to be determined by her even though in discharging that duty she might be expected to consult with local authority and other interests concerned. If, however, the central funds were provided collectively by the local authorities through a modified pooling system the National Body would have a responsibility to the Secretary of State and towards local authorities collectively and it would be appropriate for a substantial part of the membership to be nominated by the local authority associations, and for a further proportion to be nominated by the Secretary of State in recognition of her overall responsibility for the effectiveness of the education service.

5.22. Some of our members had serious misgivings about modified pooling and considered that only direct grant would provide a funding arrangement which was uncomplicated, economic and accountable. Our local authority members, however, left us in no doubt as to the importance they attach to central government's financial contribution to local authority expenditure being to the greatest extent possible through a block grant like the present Rate Support Grant and not earmarked for particular items of expenditure. For these reasons and because in general an evolution of the present pooling system would, they thought, be more acceptable to the local authority world than more radical change, we felt bound after carefully balancing the arguments to discard the alternative of direct grant and to prefer alternative (c).

5.23. Before committing ourselves finally to this alternative we needed to assure ourselves that:

(a) a system of joint local and national finance supplemented by substantial fee income, however acceptable in theory, would not be found too complicated to function satisfactorily in practice; in this connection we were at pains to ensure that suitable arrangements could be made to deal with the large number of authorities and institutions with widely varying involvement in higher education without unduly burdensome administration;

(b) direct contributions from individual maintaining authorities could be fixed at a level which would permit an effective system of joint finance without imposing an intolerable burden on smaller authorities making substantial higher education provision.

5.24. We defer to Chapter VII our examination of the financial mechanisms which could be employed to meet the possible difficulties referred to at (a) above and will here only anticipate our conclusions to say (i) that we are satisfied that a system of joint finance could be effective without unduly cumbersome administration, and (ii) that the proposed National Body should be free to determine its own methods of operation which we should not attempt to lay down in advance. In the next section we discuss the question of the relative proportions of local and national finance and the impact of a direct local contribution on the financial position of individual maintaining authorities.

The Local Contribution

5.25. As we have already made clear we attach importance to the principle that responsibility for management decisions should be accompanied by appropriate financial responsibility. We believe that a system under which all finance for maintained higher education was provided centrally by the National Body would inevitably reduce the maintaining authorities to the role of mere agents for the provision of higher education and would bring in question whether the continuance of a maintained sector of higher education was desirable at all. However, having accepted that local education authorities will retain a significant role in the provision of higher education, it follows that this should be accompanied by a corresponding financial responsibility.

5.26. We should perhaps make clear at this point that whatever proportion was chosen for the share of costs to be borne by individual maintaining authorities it would be an average for the system as a whole and individual authorities would in practice generally pay more or less. There are important reasons why this should be so. First, it is no part of our proposals that the National Body should have power to direct local authorities in relation to their higher education provision. In general, it will need to proceed by negotiation and with the agreement of individual authorities. In some cases, it may judge it right to take a relatively generous view of the level of expenditure to be supported nationally; in other cases, it must be able to withhold or reduce financial support for activities it regards as unnecessary or uneconomic. In the latter case it would be open to the maintaining authority to decide whether the provision should continue and make available the additional funds. Secondly, we think it important that institutions should not be rigidly bound to programmes approved by the National Body and that there should be room for local discretion. Some times this could be accommodated from savings in the approved budget, in others additional funds could be provided by the maintaining authority. Finally, and we revert to this point in a later chapter, we think it important that the system should provide adequate incentives to prudent local management. The resulting savings should accrue to the maintaining authority in relief of its contribution or be carried forward for the use of the institution itself.

5.27. While accepting the principle of a local contribution our local authority members have been anxious lest the financial effects for some maintaining authorities should be so severe as to undermine their commitment to providing higher education or render our recommendations unacceptable to the local authority world as a whole. At first sight this may appear surprising in that our recommendations involve only the redistribution between authorities of at most some £60m annually compared with total local authority current expenditure of over £12,000m. Nevertheless, closer examination shows that in a very few exceptional cases our proposals could involve an authority in a considerable financial burden unless steps were taken to avoid this. We refer in paragraph 5.36 below to ways in which this burden may be specially alleviated.

5.28. Clearly, the acceptability of our proposals would be greatly enhanced if ways could be found of mitigating such effects. The Rate Support Grant system has among its objectives the equalisation of rate burdens and the progressive matching of the grant to past expenditure. This means that provided the changes we propose were introduced gradually over a period their effects on individual authorities would be minimised by offsetting changes in the assistance they receive from Rate Support Grant.

5.29. The National Body will, in any case, need time to introduce the radical changes we envisage; this is considered in more detail in Chapter VII. Advantage might be taken of this to introduce local contributions at a low rate, say 5 per cent, initially with annual increases thereafter, subject to a review before going beyond 10 per cent. Another possibility, which we discuss in our next section on pooling arrangements, would be to make a transitional adjustment to the pooling formula which could mitigate the additional burdens falling on individual authorities over a longer period.

Pooling

5.30. Our recommendation is that national funds for maintained higher education should be provided by local authorities collectively (paragraph 5.22). At present this is done through a higher education pool to which all local education authorities contribute in accordance with a formula.

5.31. It is for local education authorities themselves to determine how in future the incidence of providing national funds should be apportioned between them. In this contect our interest is confined to ensuring that our recommendations for joint national and local finance need not place such additional financial burdens on individual maintaining authorities as to render them unacceptable. There appear to be two possibilities which would merit examination:

(a) whether an alternative pooling formula could be found which was justifiable on its own merits and which would at the same time mitigate the financial burden which would otherwise, under a system of joint finance, fall on certain maintaining authorities, and

(b) whether a transitional adjustment could be made to the present pooling formula which would temper the effect the joint finance where it might be unduly severe.

5.32. Under the particular formula now in use contributions are based partly (31 per cent) on an authority's share of national non-domestic rateable value and partly (69 per cent) on its share of national school population. This arrangement dates from 1975 when the previously separate teacher training and advanced further education (AFE) pools were amalgamated. Contributions to these pools had been calculated differently (the former on school population alone and the latter half by reference to school population and half by reference to non-domestic rateable value) and the choice of the 31/69 ratio was intended, so far as was practicable, to reproduce at that time the same distribution of cost as would have obtained if the amalgamation had not taken place.

5.33. The amalgamation of the pools and the revised formula for contributions conceals a difference in rationale in the formulae previously used, which should be noted. On the one hand, school population was used for the teacher training pool as a measure of the benefit which an LEA might be expected to derive from the output of the system (non-domestic rateable value was intended to provide a similar measure in the AFE pool of the benefit which local industry and commerce might derive from the output of the system). By contrast, school population was included in the AFE formula as a measure of the demand that an LEA, in terms of students from its area, might make on the system itself.

5.34. The great contraction of teacher education since the two pools were merged means that the particular formula now in use no longer has any particular justification. More generally, the use of non-domestic rateable value as a measure of the value derived from the output of the system has also lost validity through the development of AFE far beyond the bounds of commercial and technical education and the fact that its products go into a very wide range of occupations including, notably, the public services.

5.35. In principle, it seemed to us that a more equitable division of cost would result from a formula relating contributions to the number of students from each local education authority following advanced courses. A preliminary examination of this possibility showed that whatever its theoretical merits it would involve a very substantial redistribution of cost and would not offer any particular benefit to those local authorities who would be adversely affected by a system of joint local and central finance. An important cause of this effect is that abandonment of non-domestic rateable value as one of the factors in the formula would much reduce the share of the Inner London Education Authority, which has within its boundaries some 25 per cent of all non-domestic rateable value in England and Wales.

5.36. Whether or not a new formula is adopted and whatever any such new formula may be, the local contribution (even if its introduction is phased as suggested below) could cause unacceptable immediate increases in the contributions to the cost of higher education from some authorities. Any such unacceptably sharp redistribution of the cost of higher education could however be mitigated by a temporary transitional adjustment to the contribution formula. It would thus be possible for arrangements to ensure that initially the total contribution to the cost of higher education from any LEA (direct and via the pool) was kept within any desired degree of proximity to the total contribution before the introduction of the new system. It would however be an essential part of the arrangements that no further adjustments should be made to take account of developments following the introduction of joint finance. Failure to observe this principle

21

would erode the purpose of local contributions and the benefits that might be expected from their introduction. The length of the period during which the system should continue to protect LEAs should be considered in the light of experience of its working and as part of a general review.

Conclusions

5.37. Any changes in the arrangements for pooling, whether involving a new basis for calculating contributions or the introduction of a transitional adjustment of the sort postulated above, would require more detailed consideration than we have been able to give them. We recommend that a study should be made by the Pooling Committee of alternative formulae for determining contributions to the pool and of possible transitional arrangements designed to mitigate difficulties arising from the introduction of local contributions.

5.38. The Rate Support Grant system should, however, over a time mitigate the additional financial burdens which will fall on maintaining authorities from the system of dual finance we recommend; further mitigation might be effected by adjustments to the pooling arrangements. We think therefore that a local contribution not greater than 15 per cent of net expenditure should not cause difficult financial problems to any maintaining authority. We recommend, however, that it should be introduced by stages. In the first year in which joint finance operated the local contribution should be 5 per cent; it should be raised to 10 per cent in the second year and remain at that level in year three. During year three its effects should be reviewed in the light of the Pooling Committee's study of alternative pooling arrangements and the National Body should make recommendations in the light of the new system's operation during the first two years to the Department and the local authority associations on further increases to a maximum level of 15 per cent.

CHAPTER VI

Constitution, Composition and Staff of the National Body

6.1. The arrangements we propose will entrust the National Body with an important executive role. It will need an independent Chairman who is prepared to devote at least a substantial part of his time to its affairs, and it might be better particularly in the earlier years if he were full-time. It will also be necessary for individual members to devote a substantial part of their time to the Body's work, and this will have to be taken into account by those who nominate persons for appointment.

6.2. The National Body must be sufficiently small to enable it to carry out its task effectively. We think therefore that it should not have more than 25 to 30 members. Within this compass it must include elected members and officers from the local authority world, persons from the management and staff of the higher education institutions they maintain, independent academics and members from schools and the world of employment. If the National Body is to command the confidence of those concerned it will need to be seen to be widely representative; on the other hand, if it is to develop a corporate identity its members must be free to form their own judgements and should serve in a personal capacity, not as delegates of those interests which in a sense they represent.

6.3. After much consideration, we think a Body constituted as follows would best satisfy these considerations. All members would be appointed by the Secretary of State, each for a fixed period renewable; they would consist of:

  (i) an independent Chairman selected by the Secretary of State

 (ii) 8 to 9 members nominated by the local authority associations

(iii) 8 institutional members including
      3 nominated by the National Association of Teachers in Further and Higher Education (NATFHE)
      2 nominated by the Committee of Directors of Polytechnics (CDP)
      3 nominated by the Secretary of State after consultation with or in the light of suggestions from organisations representing management or staff of maintained institutions providing higher education

 (iv) 8 to 10 members nominated by the Secretary of State to provide in particular for representation of the academic world including universities, schools, and commerce and industry, and to enable individuals to be appointed who by virtue of their abilities and experience could contribute to the work of the National Body.

The Department should be represented by assessors. If, as we have suggested, the remit of the National Body is extended to include responsibility for advising the Secretary of State on the plans of voluntary colleges and on their financial support, the proposed membership of the National Body will need also to reflect the interests of the voluntary providing bodies and their institutions.

6.4. A Body constituted as above would be tri-partite, consisting of approximately equal numbers from local authorities, institutions and elsewhere. About half of its members would be nominated by individual organisations and about half by the Secretary of State. We recommend that the Secretary of State should consult widely before deciding on her nominations and that there should also be mutual consultations between her and the nominating bodies in order to ensure that the best balance of knowledge and expertise is made available to the National Body.

6.5. Our proposal for the number of members to be nominated by the local authority associations is designed to provide eight members from England and a ninth member from Wales, should the National Body have responsibility for Welsh higher education (see Chapter XI).

6.6. Our recommendation that three institutional members should be nominated by the Secretary of State reflects the fact that a considerable number of organisations besides the NATFHE and CDP have some claim to be represented on the National Body. Such claims would be ruled out by the limited number of places available and we would expect the Secretary of State to select her three nominees on their merits from suggestions put forward by all those concerned, including, if they so wished, NATFHE and CDP also. Care should be taken to ensure that within the total of eight institutional members there is at least one principal of a non-polytechnic institution substantially involved in higher education.

6.7. The third element of members nominated by the Secretary of State will have, inter alia, to remedy any gaps in experience or knowledge which may be left by other nominations; on some occasions for this purpose (for example, to ensure the availability of adequate financial expertise) or to provide a good geographical balance one or two of her nominees might best be persons from local authorities or institutions. For these reasons we have felt it desirable to recommend that the Secretary of State should have some discretion in the number of members she might nominate.

Special Provision for Local Authority Members

6.8. Our local authority members have represented to us that local authorities being responsible for the provision of maintained higher education and for meeting a substantial part of its cost will be in a special position in relation to the National Body. We accept the force of this argument but think that it would be helpful to the good working of the National Body if local authority membership were not increased to an extent which would give them a dominating voice. We think it better to preserve the tri-partite composition we have recommended above and to safeguard the position of the local authorities in another way. We recommend therefore that if the local authority members are on any occasion united in relation to a particular matter under consideration and find themselves in a minority they should, if

24

they so wish, be able to require that the National Body should refrain from a decision and instead refer the matter to the Secretary of State to decide in consultation with the local authority associations. This procedure would only be operative if brought into effect by unanimity among the local authority members present.

6.9. We believe that this safeguard would reflect the reality that the National Body could not, whatever its theoretical powers, administer the system of management we have recommended without a sufficient measure of support from the local authority world generally. We think that, in practice, the safeguard would be rarely, if ever, invoked, but that its very existence would provide a powerful and effective protection to local authorities against action by the National Body which did not command in sufficient measure their assent.

6.10. We have already noted that members of the National Body will need to be able to devote a substantial part of their time to its work. We do not think that a widespread practice of representation by alternates would be desirable. Nevertheless, persons of the calibre required will inevitably have other important duties. We recommend therefore that the Secretary of State and organisations nominating members should also be able to nominate a strictly limited number of persons who would be appointed by the Secretary of State as alternates and would receive all papers of the Body.

6.11. The National Body will require staff adequate in number and calibre to carry out its substantial responsibilities. We recommend that they should be employed by the National Body itself which, if necessary, should be a body corporate. In practice, we would expect most to be recruited (eg on secondment) from the Department, local authorities and individual institutions; for example, the Further Education Advisory Team recently set up by the Council of Local Education Authorities might be linked with the National Body's work. Pending legislation (see Chapter XII) the cost of the National Body should be met by the Department but the latter should consider with the local authority associations whether the legislation should provide for the cost to be met from the modified pool we have recommended.

CHAPTER VII

Control and Finance of Higher Education Programmes and Courses

7.1. In this section we examine the practicability of a joint system of national and local finance, the methods which the National Body might adopt in allocating its finance and some general principles which might inform a system of shared finance.

7.2. We are, however, agreed that we should not lay down in advance and in detail the methods of operation which the National Body should employ. The latter should be free, once it is established, to determine these for itself in consultation with the local authority associations and other interested organisations. What is said in this chapter, which records our views on the matter, is subject to that caveat.

A Variety of Mechanisms

7.3. Higher education in the maintained sector is provided in a large number and wide range of institutions and it would, clearly, be impracticable to suggest that the National Body should concern itself in detail with the provision and budgets of all of them. It will therefore need a variety of styles and mechanisms appropriate to varying types of institution and provision, which will enable it to exercise overall control of the system, without involving it in undue detail. We identified three possible financial mechanisms:

  (a) per capita payments,
  (b) payments for individual courses, and
  (c) finance on the basis of total higher education programmes.

Per Capita Finance

7.4. We envisage that any authority should be eligible to receive national financial support for its higher education provision on the basis of per capita payments for each student depending on the type of course being pursued. Such a system would, however, be particularly suitable for courses designed to meet local and regional needs and for courses which formed a small part of the work of an institution mainly engaged in non-advanced further education.

7.5. The per capita payments would be determined by the National Body, perhaps initially on the basis of average costs for various categories of course but ultimately on agreed norms designed, in the case of reasonably cost-effective institutions whose courses recruited viable numbers, to meet 85 to 95 per cent of the total net cost, dependent upon the level agreed at the time for the local contribution. The fact that the remainder of the cost was met by maintaining authorities would provide them with an incentive to rationalise provision and avoid proliferation of competing courses. The regional advisory councils (RACs) proposed in Chapter IX would be the main agents for promoting this rationalisation and advising on proposals for new courses, but, provided the process was monitored and the level of per capita payments adjusted from time to time if the provision of courses appeared to get out of line with demand, we think the present formal system of course approvals could be discontinued (cf paragraph 9.8).

Course Finance

7.6. Where a maintaining authority felt that national finance on a per capita basis could endanger the continuance of a course which appeared to be required on national or regional grounds, because the burden of cost falling on its rate payers was excessive, it would be open to it to propose to the National Body that it should receive financial support for the course as a whole. This might be based on agreed estimates of cost adjusted annually in the light of experience or more simply in some cases by guaranteeing per capita payments for a minimum number of students irrespective of how many were actually recruited. It would be an essential corollary of this form of support that the course should be approved by the National Body. We do not envisage that approval and finance of individual courses would be appropriate for a major part of the total provision but we would regard it as suited to individual courses of national or regional importance in institutions mainly engaged in non-advanced work.

Programme Finance

7.7. Major institutions offering a substantial volume of higher education pose problems of a rather different kind, and we believe that LEAs responsible for their maintenance may well be expected to apply to the National Body for an annual contribution based on the totality of their higher education provision (model (c) above).

7.8. Three considerations, in particular, lead us to make this suggestion. First, it is increasingly recognised that the activities of institutions with a substantial involvement in higher education need to be examined as a whole. Secondly, with the development of modular and interdisciplinary courses and the growing interdependence of course structures generally control of individual courses is less and less a satisfactory way of managing higher education. Thirdly, LEAs which maintain high cost institutions could find themselves in severe financial difficulties if national support for their institutions took the form of per capita finance. It is important that unacceptably high costs should be reduced but this will have to be done gradually and with care if damage is not to be done to an institution's long-term viability.

7.9. For major institutions and particularly those for whom per capita finance would place an unacceptable burden on the maintaining authority we think therefore that the option of a system of programme finance and control should be available. Under this the National Body's financial contribution would be based on estimates covering an institution's total expenditure and a programme covering its whole education provision (with appropriate allowance made for costs attributable to any non-advanced further education). Once the estimates and the programme had been agreed the institution

27

would have considerable discretion in applying the approved funds within broad heads and in varying the detailed provision of courses and students to be recruited within specified areas and levels of work. It would, however, in so doing be expected to consult with and take into account the views of neighbouring institutions whose provision might be adversely affected by such changes; this consultation would be handled under the regional advisory councils recommended in Chapter IX.

7.10. The principal instrument in assessing the national contribution to the financing of institutions operating under a system of programme finance and control would be rolling development plans, which would incorporate estimates of expenditure for three to five years ahead analysed by departments and appropriate categories of overhead expenditure, together with forecasts of staff and student numbers in the various education areas.

7.11. Each institution would be responsible in the first instance for the preparation of such plans and estimates and for their submission to the maintaining authority. The latter would forward them to the National Body after scrutiny and any necessary modification, having decided how far it was prepared to support them through the local contribution from its own resources; in doing so it would indicate to the National Body any changes which were not agreed with the institution. It would also send copies to the regional advisory council for information and comment (paragraph 9.7).

7.12. It would be for the National Body to decide, having before it any advice and comment received from the RAC, how far these plans and estimates were acceptable, in the light of its views on national priorities, the appropriate level of costs for such institutions and any special circumstances. It would discuss with the institution and its LEA modifications which it thought necessary, eg to curtail activities judged unlikely to become cost-effective as well as to initiate developments in other areas to meet perceived national needs. Finally, it would fix for the following year, and on an indicative basis only for subsequent years, limits of expenditure on which it would make a national contribution at the appropriate percentage.

7.13. While the formal annual procedure would be as indicated above we would expect that in practice on many matters institutions would deal directly with the National Body, and the annual procedure would be supplemented by informal consultations between the parties at more frequent intervals.

7.14. In principle, the National Body's contribution once determined would be a fixed sum. Provision might, however, be made for supplementation to meet inflation in accordance with predetermined rules or, alternatively, a margin might be included at the outset for this purpose within an overall cash limit. To provide an incentive to prudent manangement and to encourage financial responsibility, savings which arose as a result of effective management and which were not fortuitous or the result simply of a failure to implement the approved programme should accrue to the authority in reduction of its share of the total cost or to the institution itself for the carrying forward to a future year.

7.15. Although we would expect programme finance to apply generally to the whole of an institution's higher education provision this need not necessarily be the case and some authorities might prefer particular faculties or areas of work to receive programme finance, the rest receiving per capita finance. This would, however, be for the National Body to decide in each case, and it would, no doubt, wish to ensure that this course was not adopted soley to maximise an LEA's entitlement to national support.

7.16. We have considered whether we should suggest detailed criteria for determining which and how many institutions might be accepted for programme finance and control. We decided not to do so because, as with the rest of the matters covered in this chapter, it would be for the National Body itself to evolve criteria in the light of experience. Considerations of workload and the need to avoid too large a bureaucracy would also, no doubt, limit the total number of such institutions which the National Body could finance in this way. We would suggest, however, as a general proposition, that to be eligible for programme finance and control institutions should have a high degree of involvement in higher education and provide courses of national rather than of purely local or regional importance. Furthermore, we attach importance to the principle that institutions of similar character and in similar circumstances should be eligible for similar treatment.

Possible Transfer of Institutions to National Control.

7.17. It would run counter to our concept of partnership between national and local interest to recommend any general transfer of institutions from local to national control. We are, however, aware of the view, which was expressed in some of the evidence submitted to us, that certain institutions by their size and complexity are natural candidates for national rather than local control, and there are circumstances in which we ourselves think individual transfers might be beneficial and some institutions (including some existing voluntary and direct grant institutions) might become a more direct responsibility of the National Body in terms of financing and control.

7.18. This would, however, be a development dependent in each case on a proposal from the relevant maintaining authority (or providing body) and on the agreement of the National Body. Moreover, it should not be a haphazard process but should only involve institutions subject to or eligible for programme finance, which the National Body in the light of its experience of the operation of the system as a whole considered to be appropriate candidates for transfer.

7.19. Subject to this, we envisage that it should be open to an LEA to propose to the National Body that it should assume responsibility for the direct control of and ultimate authority over an institution. The LEA would have a right to continue to appoint the governing body and to be consulted about the institution's current and forward plans before decisions were taken on them by the National Body, and would have first claim on any surplus accommodation in the institution for non-advanced FE on a repayment basis. In return, it would continue to make a contribution to the estimated running costs of the institution. But this contribution, like that of the National Body under normal programme finance, would be calculated at the start of each year as a percentage of an agreed estimate and would not be subject to adjustment to reflect any changes in the institution's expenditure subsequently during the course of the year. The LEA's financial liability would be limited and the National Body would assume its role in relation to financial control, meeting any excess costs or benefitting from savings.

7.20. An agreement on these lines might provide for a review after a period of, say, five years and it would be open to the National Body to impose conditions to be fulfilled before the transfer could take place: for example, that certain modifications should be made to the institution's forward plans or that certain areas of work should be discontinued. The National Body might also require that the authority's contribution should be at a level which recognised abnormal costs. Finally, it would be necessary for appropriate arrangements to be agreed at the outset between the National Body and the authority in respect of the physical assets of the institution and the formal status of the staff; this might require the institution to be transformed from a maintained establishment into a corporate body.

7.21. We believe that the three alternative mechanisms which we have described in paragraphs 7.4–7.16 above should normally be adequate either individually or in combination to meet the needs of any local education authority or institution. As a minimum all would be eligible to receive financial support on the basis of per capita finance and the maintaining authority would then be free from any central control. Where because of high cost, the national importance of the educational provision in question, or for other reasons, the maintaining authority wished to receive special support in the form of course or programme finance it would be free to apply to the National Body which would determine in the light of discussions with the authority whether such support was justified and on what conditions it might be available. Finally, as an additional possibility, an authority who so wished could ask the National Body to take over responsibility for the maintenance of its institution in return for a fixed annual contribution towards its running costs.

7.22. We believe that given this variety of possibilities the normal processes of discussion and negotiation should serve to resolve any differences between the National Body and individual local education authorities, and that the need to protect national funds provided collectively by all local education authorities should not prejudice the interests of individual authorities maintaining higher education institutions.

7.23. We have set out in paragraphs 7.10–7.13 the procedures which would be followed in the National Body's dealings with authorities and institutions. The preparation of plans must be undertaken initially by the institutions although the need for early consultation with the LEA on such matters as the impact of their plans on those of other institutions and their resource implications must be emphasised. The National Body may wish to discuss the plans with an LEA but will not have the power to force on an LEA expenditure from the authority's resources which it is not prepared to accept. In particular, the National Body might wish to develop a particular initiative (eg to locate in a particular institution a course in one of the rare technologies) or to suggest some bigger project than had been submitted to it. If, however, the LEA was unwilling to accept its share of the additional expenditure involved, the normal recourse of the National Body would be to seek to locate it elsewhere. Only in the most extreme cases would a disagreement reach the point where the LEA might wish to consider the fall-back device under which it would suggest that the institution should transfer to the National Body's control.

National Body: Cycle of Operations

7.24. The tasks which we have outlined for the National Body in the previous chapter, and certain aspects of which we have tried to fill out in this chapter, will be substantial. They will also have to be carried out so as to interlock with activities (such as the RSG negotiations and local authority budgeting) over whose timing the National Body will have no control. We have therefore examined the practicability of reconciling the system we propose with these external constraints.

7.25. A note describing the procedures for pooling at present and the arrangements which might be involved under our proposals for a modified pool under the control of the National Body is attached as Appendix C to this report. A possible annual cycle of the National Body's decision-making procedures might be as follows:

(i) Analysis of trends of unit costs and student numbers with a view to formulating advice to the Secretary of State and the local authority associations on the level of national provision for higher education in the next but one financial year and succeeding financial years. *December–March*

(ii) Discussion of this advice between central government and local authority associations, leading to their determination of national provision for the subsequent financial year in the context of the RSG settlement and indicative figures for later years. *April–November*

(iii) (concurrently with (ii)) Formal call for forecast estimates from local authorities in respect of institutions eligible for programme finance or of students in various categories on the basis of indicative figures as announced the previous November. *July–September*

(iv) Call for revisions to estimates submitted under (iii) in the light of the latest figures for national provision announced following (ii). *November*

(v) Final decisions on national financial contribution to the cost of individual institutions and on the level of per capita payments (and limits on student numbers in various categories) for the academic year and, on an indicative basis, for the following four years. *(Year 2) December–January*

We think that a timetable on these lines, modified if necessary in the light of experience, should enable the National Body to synchronise its decisions with the timetable applicable to central and local government financial procedures. We should perhaps make it clear that much work of the National Body will be conducted over a longer timescale and at a different rhythm. Many annual decisions would be little more than confirmation of agreements reached in discussions over a longer period about either the programmes of individual institutions, or total provision country-wide in a particular educational area.

Phased Introduction of New System

7.26. The system of management and financial control outlined above could as a matter of practice only be introduced over a period. We have already recommended in Chapter V that, to mitigate the additional financial burdens falling on particular maintaining authorities from its introduction, the local contribution should be raised to 15 per cent by stages. We think that the full system might be introduced over five years under the following timetable:

Year 1. (after the National Body has become fully operational) Limitation of pooling to 95 per cent of net expenditure. Determination of per capita payments for various categories of courses. Preparation by local education authorities with institutions predominantly engaged in higher education of proposals for programme financing and control.

Year 2. Limitation of pooling to 90 per cent. First application of per capita payments. Examination of proposals for programme finance.

Year 3. Review of effects of introduction of local contributions to cost and determination of timetable for further possible increases in their amount. Introduction of programme finance and control for selected high cost institutions.

Year 4. Extension of programme finance and control to further institu-
and 5. tions.

Practicability of a Joint System of Finance

7.27. We observed at the start of this chapter that our aim in considering the detailed operation of a joint system of national and local finance was not to prescribe the methods which the National Body should employ but to satisfy ourselves as to its practicability. We believe that we have done this. The system finally adopted by the National Body may differ in detail or in substance from that which we have outlined in this chapter, but we believe that it need not be unduly complicated or cumbersome to operate and could preserve a considerable degree of local autonomy within an overall framework of national control.

CHAPTER VIII

Management at Local Level

8.1. The new system of management and financial control which we have recommended will in no way diminish the responsibility of individual maintaining authorities for the good management of their institutions. On the one hand, it will clarify the educational objectives and their place in national plans, and, on the other, set clear limits on the extent to which the cost may be met from national funds. This will be accompanied by the discontinuance generally of controls over individual courses, giving maintaining authorities wider discretion in obtaining the agreed objectives under financial arrangements offering a direct incentive to efficient management.

8.2. It is accepted policy that maintaining authorities should share their overall responsibility for the running of their institutions with the institutions themselves. The Education (No. 2) Act 1968 requires each institution to have a governing body appointed by the LEA and to be conducted in accordance with articles of government approved by the Secretary of State which determine the functions to be exercised by the education authority, the governing body, the principal and the academic board. Despite this provision there is, however, a wide variety in the way in which institutions are in practice managed, and it is a common complaint, reflected in evidence submitted to us, that some local authorities intervene in the detailed management of their institutions so as effectively to prevent governing bodies from exercising the responsibilities for management entrusted to them by their institution's articles of government.

8.3. We fully support the emphasis which the Department's guidance[1] places on institutions being granted the maximum freedom to manage their own affairs. We believe that it is central to good management that the power to take decisions and the associated financial responsibility should, wherever practicable, be delegated downwards. At the same time, the maintaining authority must be able to discharge its overall responsibility for the institution's effectiveness and this requires that the powers and responsibilities which are delegated should be clearly defined, so that those responsible at each level can operate with confidence in the area of their responsibility.

8.4. Maintained institutions have the legal status of establishments of the maintaining authority. Their staffs are employed and their buildings owned by the authority. During our discussions it was suggested that it would be easier for institutions to be given adequate responsibility for their own management if, like direct grant institutions, they had corporate status, employed their own staff, and owned their buildings. Others would take a different view and we decided not to pursue this possibility since we considered, as a Group, that a formal distinction in status is less important than the ability of an institution,

---

[1]Notes for Guidance on the Government and Academic Organisation of Polytechnics (Administrative Memorandum 8/67 (1967)) and Circular 7/70 on the Government and Conduct of Establishments of Further Education (1970).

whatever its status, to operate within clearly defined powers and limitations. We return to this in paragraph 8.14 below.

8.5.   In considering how the required powers and limitations could best be defined we have separated the question into

(a) the external relationship between the institution and its parent local education authority, and

(b) internal relationships within the institution between the governing body, academic board, director and other staff responsible for its good management.

But a common factor in considering both these facets is our belief that the governing body of an institution must be constituted and allowed to operate in such a way as to provide a clear focus of authority and accountability. This should be emphasised by the practice recommended in Circular 7/70 of entrusting its business to a clerk directly responsible to it (normally the chief administrative officer of the college) while according the chief education officer of the maintaining LEA the right to receive papers and to attend and speak at meetings of the governing body as necessary.

Relationship between the Governing Body and Local Education Authority

8.6. We start from the principle that the maintaining authority should be responsible for determining, in the context of the national system already outlined, the general character and educational role of its institution and establishing the budget within which it must operate. Subject to this, we take the view that institutions and their governing bodies should be accorded the greatest practicable degree of operational freedom in matters relating to

(a) the appointment of all grades of staff, including non-teaching staff, and

(b) purchases and contracts.

8.7. On staffing, we consider that the retention of detailed establishment control by the maintaining LEA is unreasonable and may be uneconomic. The aim should therefore be to give governing bodies prime responsibility for determining the establishment and grading of both their teaching and non-teaching staff within a ceiling on total numbers and within an overall budget, with the decisions to be taken annually by the maintaining LEA limited to

(a) the determination of the total sums for teaching staff and non-teaching staff expenditure (with suitable provision for virement between them), and

(b) so long as a policy of manpower ceilings obtains, the determination of the maximum numbers of staff to be employed in the two categories.

It is important to emphasise that the LEA would not lay down any actual establishment for the institution, either globally or by grades (although until and unless some alternative method may be devised, the figures included in an institution's rolling budget would be bound to reflect both existing establishments and the educational programme of the institution as agreed).

8.8. There remains, however, the complex question of the degree of freedom to be allowed to the governing body of an institution in determining the grading of staff, since we are conscious that, unless institutions already have or receive corporate status, maintaining LEAs will continue to be the employers of the staff concerned and may therefore feel a need to retain some control over certain aspects of staffing decisions to ensure comparability of treatment (in terms of pay and conditions of service) with their own staff, particularly those in similar colleges.

8.9. In some instances, grading structures and criteria are determined nationally or locally by recognised bodies and it is clear that institutions must observe the limitations of these agreements. This is not always felt, however, to be sufficient, since some aspects of the problem are not dealt with in such bodies and some authorities take the view that the range of allowable variation within negotiated agreements is such as to require some further limitation of the discretion of their governing bodies.

8.10. It seems to us that time will be required to examine and find a solution to these issues, as they affect, for example,

(a) the range of allowable variation under Burnham;

(b) the implementation of changes in grading and structure that arise as a consequence of relevant national, regional and local negotiations with recognised unions;

(c) the formulation of an agreed framework for salaries and grading of senior non-teaching staff, and

(d) the grading of junior non-teaching staff (which in the absence of national or regional agreements tends to be governed by the maintaining authority's own regulations).

In the course of this examination, it will be necessary, in particular, to determine in which areas, to ensure reasonably uniform treatment of institutions undertaking similar types of work, clear national guidelines are required.

8.11. In the interim, governing bodies must know clearly the extent of their discretion, and it will be necessary for this to be determined by maintaining LEAs and the National Body (where the latter is concerned with approving budgets). We recommend, however, that any constraints which it may be necessary for individual authorities still to apply should be general rather than detailed in character and should keep firmly in mind the principles set out in paragraph 8.6 above. The National Body should also concern itself with assisting authorities and institutions to move in this direction as quickly as may be practicable.

35

8.12. On the question of purchases and contracts, which was also referred to in paragraph 8.6, we take the view that, in general, the governing body should be free to make its own arrangements, except in a few defined areas, rather than have to make a case on each occasion it wishes to use services other than the LEA's. The obligation on the governing body must be to operate in the most cost-effective way. With this obligation, however, should go a freedom to purchase goods and services wherever the governing body considers best; often the LEA's supplies services will meet the institution's needs but sometimes they will not. A similar freedom should apply to contractual matters other than those relating to capital expenditure. Only in cases where the maintaining LEA might as a result be financially at risk should there be a need for any limitations to this freedom.

8.13. In putting forward the views expressed in the preceding paragraphs we are aware that some authorities and colleges may have difficulty in accepting our approach in full, especially as it affects staffing. Nonetheless, we think it vital that institutions which are rightly expected to demonstrate a high degree of accountability should not find themselves unnecessarily involved in the processes of an authority's corporate management structures, however important these may be for the authority's own functioning. On the other hand, we accept that we must provide for a situation, however unlikely, where a governing body acts irresponsibly or ultra vires in such a way as to allow expenditure to get out of control. To provide for extreme cases of this sort we suggest that provision be made whereby the governing body could be dissolved and arrangements made for the discharge of its functions pending the establishment of a new governing body.

Financial Arrangements and Regulations

8.14. We turn now to consider the financial arrangements under which institutions should operate. It is clear that if institutions are to enjoy greater autonomy in the running of their own affairs they must be subject to overall financial controls which may well be different from and tougher than those currently operated. Furthermore, if institutions are to be given the necessary incentives to be more efficient and financially responsible, these controls must be applied in an appropriate manner. We believe three elements to be important:

(a) the funding relationship between LEA and institution should be based on the concept of a closed budget within which the institution's expenditure must be contained. Clearly, in an era of inflation, some provision for supplementation will be necessary but this should be on the basis of predetermined rules (cf paragraph 7.14);

(b) institutions should be able to carry over to the next year at least some part of any savings which may have accrued as a result of their efficient operation, if necessary under specified heads. Such monies should be available for financing activities for which funds may not be available within their approved budgets for the following year but which fall within the general framework of their agreed development programmes;

36

(c) financial planning and control should be on the basis of rolling programmes covering the current year and at least two subsequent years, in accordance with the pattern established by the National Body for its own purposes.

8.15. No doubt there will have to be a transition period covering the change to a regime in which the governing body has greater freedom to operate within a fixed budget. We recommend that the National Body should have, as a prime task, to generate sufficient guidance, in consultation with the local authority associations, to facilitate this process.

8.16. We have not been able to consider in detail all aspects of the relationship between an institution and its LEA and these will need careful examination. They are too complex to be incorporated in articles of government and financial regulations will have to be drawn up to govern the funding of an institution. These might include:

a. *General*

    i. submission of estimates and other documentation in a form prescribed and approved by the LEA.

    ii. accounting and audit requirements, including presentation of financial documents in a prescribed form, and provisions relating to fee income and other resources not covered by grant.

    iii. definition of authorised expenditure and of the extent of virement allowed both within and between heads of expenditure.

    iv. supplementation—limitations on, definitions of and methods of application for such grants.

    v. VAT and other taxation obligations: methods of payment and claiming.

b. *Revenue expenditure and income*

    i. staffing (both teaching and non-teaching) establishments, rates of pay, conditions of service—controls and conditions. Methods of calculation and determination of resource allocations.

    ii. goods, services and materials: expenditure heads and limitations.

    iii. appointment of advisers, contractors etc: limitations on such appointments and rates of pay.

    iv. research, consultancy and other income: contribution towards overheads, eg support staffing and/or other costs.

    v. balances and the holding of accumulated funds; trading operations; full cost courses, and investment.

    vi. residential and catering operations.

c. *Capital and other specially authorised expenditure*

    i. definitions (eg between major and minor capital works programmes); methods of seeking approval to major capital expenditure, controls, approvals and payments.

ii. minor works controls.

iii. technical and other major equipment; programme and specific approvals.

We recommend that careful consideration be given to these points at an early stage.

8.17. Finally, under this section, we wish to draw attention to two issues which we have noted during our examination but which fall outside our main concern:

(a) the lack of accountability inherent in present arrangements whereby the governing bodies of institutions are generally responsible for approving student union fees, which in the case of most students attract mandatory grant, and

(b) the appropriateness or otherwise of some of the provisions of the Burnham Document to the requirements of a major higher education institution's management structure, eg the salary arrangements for senior management and the absence of any limit on the number of persons payable on the vice-principal scale and the absence of a third-tier scale between vice-principal and head of department.

We recommend that these issues should be considered further by the appropriate bodies, the first in the context of the review of student union financing which we understand to be in progress.

Internal Structures

8.18. We turn now to the question of internal structures and, in particular, to consider the respective roles and functions of the governing body, the academic board and the principal. The model articles of government appended to Circular 7/70 defined these as follows:

(a) the governors shall be responsible for the general direction of the college.

(b) the principal shall be responsible to the governors for the internal organisation, management and discipline of the college, and

(c) subject to the overall responsibilities of the governors, the academic board shall be responsible for the planning, coordination, development and oversight of the academic work of the college, including arrangements for the admission and examination of students.

8.19. These provisions were designedly in general terms so as not to preclude the development in individual institutions of relationships and arrangements appropriate to their circumstances and to permit varying styles of management. It appears, however, in the light of experience of their working, that the under-lying principles tend to be obscured and management arrangements have developed which inhibit proper accountability and blur responsibilities. In our view, it is desirable that there should be further clarification of the respective roles of the governing body, academic board and principal; in particular, since a large part of the expenditure of any higher education institution is related to academic matters and there is bound to be a close relationship between academic and financial responsibilities, it is important to avoid confusion between the powers of the academic board and the governing body and to establish a proper relationship between them. We return in paragraph 8.29 below to the question of formulating further guidance.

Governing Body

8.20. We wish to emphasise that the governing body is ultimately responsible to the LEA for all expenditure on the running of its institution; it was on this assumption that we recommended above that it should be accorded greater autonomy. In exercising this responsibility it will, no doubt, as a matter of practice, delegate authority to the principal, who may in turn wish to delegate authority for expenditure in particular areas to his deputies, heads of faculty or department or other subordinate officers, but it should be clearly understood that in exercising such authority they do so on behalf of the governing body. The academic board, on the other hand, or its sub-committees may well make recommendations which have expenditure implications but it has to be understood that the authority for deciding on them must remain vested in those who are responsible for the management of the institution, and this principle should not be eroded. It may be that to make the relationship between governing body and academic board clearer than it may have been in the past, articles should in future be fuller than hitherto.

8.21. We believe that clarification of their functions on these lines together with a granting of greater autonomy by LEAs are recommended in paragraph 8.6 will assist members of governing bodies to acquire a sense of corporate identity and full responsibility for the running of their institution. But it is important also to see that such bodies' constitution and modus operandi are appropriate and in this connection we wish to draw attention, in particular, to the following points:

(a) the arrangements for the appointment of non-staff members of the governing body must be such as to ensure continuity of membership and to enable them to acquire an adequate insight into the institution's operations.

(b) members of the governing body should be associated through sub-committees and otherwise with specific areas of the institution's work. Provision is already made for the establishment of finance sub-committees and we also, in particular, recommend the practice of establishing a joint committee of governing body and academic board with responsibility for forward planning.

(c) the constitution of the governing body should be such as to provide a reasonable balance between representatives of the maintaining authority, representatives of internal institutional interests and independent members. This has implications not only for the

39

governing body's composition but also for the establishment of a quorum at its meetings and the membership of its various sub-committees.

We recommend that further consideration should be given to these matters. We return to this in paragraphs 8.29–30 below.

Academic Board

8.22. The academic board is, under the model articles, generally responsible within the framework of policy laid down by the governing body for the planning, coordination, development and oversight of the academic work of the college. In particular, it must be responsible for all purely academic decisions: for example, for

(a) the academic content of courses submitted to external validating bodies;

(b) decisions on admission qualifications, and

(c) academic matters relating to examinations.

Clear statements of such functions are essential.

8.23. On the other hand, in its role of planning the development of the academic work of the college and in matters which would involve expenditure not already authorised the academic board can only make recommendations to the governing body. Equally, the governing body cannot normally require the adoption of an academic programme which does not have the support of the academic board, and ways and means must be found of reconciling any differences of opinion which may arise. The principal with his joint responsibility for administrative and academic matters is well placed to perform this function.

8.24. Although the tension inherent in the relationship described above can be beneficial, it has in it the seeds of conflict. Our recommendation (paragraph 8.21(b)) on the creation of joint planning committees should help to minimise this danger. In addition, we recommend that the academic board should have sufficient access to relevant financial information to ensure that its recommendations on academic matters are always taken in full knowledge of their financial implications and of the general state of the institution's finances. The corollary would be that the governing body should not take decisions on matters relating solely to expenditure without also considering, on the basis of advice from the academic board, their academic implications.

Principal

8.25. The principal is the chief academic and administrative officer of the institution. As such, he is responsible to the governing body and should be the chairman of the academic board. As noted above, he will have a major responsibility for harmonious relationships between the latter and the governing body and for ensuring that neither encroaches on the functions of the other.

8.26.   In matters involving executive action in day-to-day management it is important that there should be a clear line of authority between the governing body, the principal and his subordinate staff. The authority, including financial authority, which is delegated to the latter should also be clearly defined. Furthermore, since day-to-day management is inevitably concerned with issues coming within the purview of both academic board and governing body it is important that those responsible for it should have adequate representation on both. This should be provided for in the case of the governing body by the Instrument of Government. In the case of the academic board (whose composition in other respects is outside our terms of reference and on which our recommendations will have to be weighed against other considerations such as the need to limit its overall size) it is important that the articles of government should provide for strong representation of departmental and faculty heads and of others involved in management, so that they may be able to make a contribution not only as prominent members in their own fields but also as persons with senior management responsibility within the institution.

8.27. Deans of faculty and heads of department should enjoy a similar position vis-a-vis faculty boards and boards of studies. We recommend also that the possibility should be examined of extending the principle of an institution's right to hold funds and carry over savings (paragraph 8.14) to the faculty or departmental level. In this way each faculty or department would have a clear incentive towards greater efficiency and financial responsibility.

Further Action

8.28. Our recommendations on an institution's relationship with its LEA and on its own internal structures will require further consideration of the model articles of government appended to Circular 7/70 and of the articles of individual institutions. But we believe that clear demarcation of the governing body's powers and responsibilities vis-a-vis its maintaining authority, particularly in relation to financial matters, will require detailed provisions which would be better drawn up separately from articles to facilitate their amendment from time to time in the light of experience. As indicated at various points in this chapter, a considerable amount of detailed work and study must be undertaken.

8.29. At present, articles of all institutions engaged in the provision of full-time and sandwich FE courses have to be submitted to the Secretary of State for approval. For the future, we have considered two options:

(a) responsibility for formulation of guidance and approval of articles would rest with the National Body, or

(b) responsibility for both activities would remain with the Secretary of State who would, however, look to the National Body for advice.

We see advantage in and recommend adoption of the second alternative; this would enable common procedures covering also colleges engaged entirely or mainly in non-advanced FE to be continued.

41

8.30. The involvement of the National Body as the source of advice to the Secretary of State would, however, reflect a general responsibility for improving the management of maintained higher education as a whole. We would expect it also therefore to take a major part in promoting and bringing to a successful conclusion the various studies and discussions, the need for which we have identified at various points in this chapter. Some of these are urgent and may have to be initiated by the Department in advance of the National Body being set up but in due course it should assume responsibility for them.

CHAPTER IX

Regional Organisation and Functions

Background

9.1. Present arrangements at regional level in England take the form of nine Regional Advisory Councils (the Welsh Joint Education Committee (WJEC) covers similar functions in Wales). These were established in 1947–48 by voluntary cooperation between LEAs in their region and are financed by them, their role being to advise on and to coordinate the provision of both non-advanced and advanced further education. Their constitutions vary, as does the extent of their involvement in both advanced and non-advanced work, but important among their functions is the scrutiny of advanced course proposals (other than teacher training proposals) before submission to the Secretary of State for approval. In the case of part-time advanced courses (with the exception of some at a higher level) RACs are themselves responsible for approvals under general authority from the Secretary of State. (Some RACs also act as Regional Examining Boards.)

9.2. Prior to 1975 there was also a network of 23 Area Training Organisations (ATOs) which were responsible for the academic oversight of the work of Colleges of Education and for the coordination of teacher training facilities in their area. These were based in all but one instance on universities and included in their membership representatives of LEAs, teachers and teacher training institutions.

9.3. The ATOs were formally discontinued by the revocation of the former Teacher Training Regulations as part of the policy of integrating teacher training and other AFE under the Further Education Regulations 1975. This policy had been announced in the 1972 White Paper[1] which had also proposed the setting up of new regional committees to coordinate the provision of initial, in-service and induction training for teachers, while recognising at the same time the need for improved arrangements for the coordination in the public sector of higher education as a whole and for a review of the composition, functions and boundaries of the Regional Advisory Councils. In the period since the publication of the White Paper various proposals have been put forward—by the Advisory Committee on the Supply and Training of Teachers in 1974 for the establishment of regional coordinating committees with a role restricted to in-service and induction training and education of teachers, and by CLEA in 1975 for Further Education Advisory Councils in the Regions with functions embracing all further education—but these failed to command general acceptance and no further progress had been made by the time our Group was established. (The WJEC also put forward proposals—broadly similar to those developed by CLEA—for the cordination of further education in Wales.)

---

[1]Cmnd. 5174.

Regional Functions

9.4. One of the fundamental assumptions underlying our report is (paragraph 3.3) that there will not for some time to come, if ever, be regional assemblies in England with powers and funds which would permit an executive regional role in the management of higher education. Nevertheless it is clear from previous experience with the Regional Advisory Councils and, in relation to teacher education, the Area Training Organisations, that there are matters which can most satisfactorily be handled at some intermediate point between national and local authority level. In the following paragraphs we identify what role regional bodies might play in the context of the system of management and financial control which we have recommended in previous chapters.

9.5. We have earlier envisaged four main functions for our management system: intelligence, planning, determining the necessary provision and allocation of resources, and oversight of the implementation of plans. In each of these there is scope for a regional role. This is notably the case in relation to planning and the information to which it is related. The most effective matching of supply and demand cannot be achieved solely on a national basis; demand for part-time higher education is essentially local or regional in character and so also is other home-based study including much recurrent education. More generally our proposals attach importance to the need for local initiative in the planning process and for the wide availability of the necessary information; an important aspect of the latter is the interchange and discussion of plans at a formative stage and we believe that regional bodies should play a major role in organising this aspect of the planning process.

9.6. Regional bodies could also play a useful role by providing a forum in which those local authorities with little higher education in their own institutions together with industry and commerce could express their needs and bring their views to bear on the planning process.

9.7. The management system we recommend would embrace a variety of mechanisms for determining provision and allocating resources. Under programme finance and control considerable local discretion would remain and even though our recommendations envisage that institutions subject to programme control should be exempt from course control, we have noted in paragraph 7.9 that they should consult with and take into account the views of neighbouring institutions before making changes in their agreed programmes. This might conveniently be undertaken in the context of an appropriately established regional committee. Moreover, while regions should not be third parties to the negotiations between maintaining authorities and the National Body in which the programmes themselves are established and the central finance for them determined, they should be kept informed of the proposals on which such negotiations are based and of the decisions in which they result and should be free to offer any comment which they may think desirable.

9.8. Where national resources are allocated through per capita finance, maintaining authorities will have considerable discretion to provide courses to meet local needs, in virtue of the fact that their funds will be at risk if the provision is not economically viable. To minimise this risk and to avoid endangering the viability of existing provision we recommend that all proposals for new courses should be discussed on a regional basis, before they are instituted. We do not think there will generally be a need to retain a formal system of course approval but we would expect local authorities in their own interest generally to be guided by the recommendations of the regional body in deciding whether or not particular courses should go ahead. The provision of national funds through course finance will be dependent on the National Body's approval of the course and when this is justified on regional grounds, the regional body's views will naturally be a major factor in the decision.

Teacher Education

9.9 Previous proposals for regional coordination in this field have distinguished between initial education and training on the one hand and in-service training and induction on the other. Since the 1972 White Paper initial teacher education has been increasingly integrated with other forms of higher education both institutionally and in the structure of courses. It follows that the adjustment of provision to meet national decisions on teacher supply must be handled under the general system of higher education management we recommend, and that any regional bodies should have the same role in relation to initial teacher education in public sector institutions as they do in relation to higher education generally.

9.10. In-service education and training including induction training, though closely linked professionally and academically to initial education and training, raises very different problems of administration. Much of it will be provided outside higher education institutions, in teachers' centres and schools. The teaching profession itself, local authority advisers and others will be important partners with academic staff of institutions in making a great variety of provision, ranging from one year full-time courses leading to higher degrees and diplomas to short courses, seminars, workshops and conferences. As the Government's consultative document 'Education in Schools'[1] points out local education authorities will have the major responsibility for developing programmes of in-service education and training because of their direct responsibility for the quality of education in schools and for the complicated administrative and logistic arrangements which an expansion on the scale intended will require.

9.11. The Government's policy is that each authority should establish advisory machinery on which institutions involved in teacher training and serving teachers should both be fully represented to help in the development of plans. We recommend that similar machinery should be established at regional level to foster cooperation between individual authorities and the coordination of their plans and to develop those programmes which need to

---

[1] Cmnd. 6869 HMSO 1977.

be organised on a regional basis. Because of the scale of the problem and its essentially home-based and local nature, some of this task may more easily be handled at sub-regional level.

Universities

9.12. Recommendations in the preceding paragraphs relate to non-university higher education. But their value will be greatly enhanced if the cooperation of the universities in each region can be enlisted in what is proposed. We recognise that this must be on a voluntary basis and should in no way erode the existing relationship between the universities and the University Grants Committee. But we do not believe that planning at the regional level for the public sector can be fully effective without information about the plans of universities in the regions and the task of coordination with the university system at national level will be eased if individual universities in making their plans can take into account developments in the public sector and vice versa. Such cooperation will be particularly necessary in the field of in-service training of teachers, since universities are themselves major providers, retain a major responsibility for validating courses in other institutions and have considerable relevant experience in the coordination of provision. We believe that universities will welcome an invitation to develop further their existing cooperation and our proposals below for the constitutions of regional bodies reflect this view.

Regional Bodies

9.13. We recommend that to carry out the functions outlined above nine new regional advisory councils should be established in England; our recommendations for Wales are contained in Chapter XI. It would probably be convenient if their functions also extended to non-advanced further education but this lies outside our terms of reference and so far as higher education is concerned their functions would be to consider, promote, monitor and advise on the planning, coordination and development in the regions of higher education outside the universities, including the initial, induction and in-service education and training of teachers.

9.14. Initially, the boundaries of each region should be those of the existing Regional Advisory Councils. Modifications of these boundaries where necessary and arrangements for membership of each local education authority and of each institution in areas of overlap should be established by negotiations between the regions as soon as the councils are established.

9.15. Each council should have a governing body which should include representatives of all the interests concerned in a tri-partite composition consisting of three broad elements: (a) representatives of local education authorities and voluntary providing bodies; (b) representatives (including both management and staff) from maintained and voluntary institutions, and (c) others, including representatives of commerce and industry, schools and universities. There should be provision within this balance for coopted as well as nominated members and for representation of Her Majesty's Inspectorate in the regions as assessors. It would not be appropriate to lay down a more precise composition because the circumstances of the different regions differ widely, eg in respect of the number of authorities, universities or institutions, and because some persons, and these would be particularly valuable, may by virtue of their occupation or experience be representative of more than one category. We think that to ensure conformity with this broad pattern and reasonable uniformity between regions it would be desirable for the constitution of each governing body to be subject to the approval of the Secretary of State.

9.16. Governing bodies composed as we propose will inevitably be on the large side and we envisage that they would meet perhaps two or three times a year, mainly to receive reports from their committees, to review progress and to establish guidelines. We recommend that the councils be set up by trust deeds which would require the establishment of two main sub-committees to deal respectively with

(a) higher education, including initial teacher education, and

(b) induction and in-service training of teachers.

Each sub-committee should also have a tri-partite membership, that of the higher education committee reflecting the composition of the governing body though somewhat smaller in size. The composition of the in-service training sub-committee should, however, reflect that of the advisory committees being established by individual local authorities and would be composed of equal numbers of local authority representatives, institutional representatives, including those of universities, and members of the teaching profession in schools.

9.17. Each council will require appropriate staff under a director with overall responsibility for carrying out the work of the council in accordance with its directions. The budget of each council would be met from the funds of the member local education authorities.

CHAPTER X

Coordination with the University System

10.1. Our terms of reference require us to consider how higher education in the maintained sector can better be coordinated with higher education in the universities.

10.2. We have already made two proposals which bear on this matter. In Chapter V we recommend that the new National Body together with the University Grants Committee and the Department of Education and Science should take steps to improve information about the prospective supply of and demand for various types of higher education. In Chapter IX we recommend that universities in the regions should be invited to cooperate with the new regional councils whose establishment we recommend and that they should be represented on them.

10.3. The Government's responsibility for the universities is discharged at national level through the University Grants Committee. The creation of a National Body for the maintained sector charged with strategic control over maintained provision will improve opportunities for discussions designed to ensure that their plans develop on complementary lines and avoid over-provision or unnecessary duplication. On some occasions developments in the maintained sector will need to be modified to take account of parallel developments in the universities; on others the reverse will be required since it is important that the responsibility for adaptation to changing circumstances does not fall solely on the maintained sector.

10.4. Both the UGC and the new National Body would be advisory to the Secretary of State. We would expect however that over a period a close cooperation would emerge between them which would enable increasingly effective coordination of developments to be achieved on a voluntary basis. Should this prove insufficient it would be for the Secretary of State to determine how the matter should be resolved.

10.5. We have already noted that our proposals are designed to meet the exigencies of an era in which expansion of higher education as a whole will be much slower than in the past and the task of management will be increasingly concerned with problems of change within a relatively static total. The question of contraction and expansion in different subject areas will assume great importance in this context. The University Grants Committee already has a range of subject sub-committees to advise it and it may well be desirable for the new National Body to establish similar committees also; in that case regular contacts between corresponding committees of the two bodies could be of great value.

10.6. The fact that control over the university system is exercised nationally is not in our view likely to render the arrangements we recommend for regional cooperation and coordination either unnecessary or ineffective. Our recommendations also envisage a system of national control over the maintained sector but with room for much local initiative and autonomy. As we see it the matters on which cooperation would be valuable at regional level are precisely those which are within the discretion of individual universities or maintaining authorities (or their institutions) and we believe that increased cooperation on a voluntary basis at regional or local level both in the planning and provision of higher education and in the development of institutional initiatives (a number of successful examples of which already exist) will be seen on both sides of the binary line as a necessary and useful complement to strategic coordination at the centre.

10.7. In putting forward these proposals we believe that both the Grants Committee and the universities generally would welcome the opportunity more systematic arrangements for the management of maintained higher education would provide for developing cooperation across the binary line on a sounder and more continuing basis than has hitherto been possible. As a Group we believe that this is necessary if the resources devoted to higher education are to be used to the best advantage.

CHAPTER XI

Wales

11.1. At present maintained higher education in Wales is administered and financed as in England. The same Further Education Regulations apply and the cost is charged to a common higher education pool.

11.2. There is, however, one significant difference in the existence of the Welsh Joint Education Committee (WJEC), a statutory body which has no counterpart in England. The Order for the establishment of the WJEC under Part II of Schedule I of the Education Act of 1944 provides that the WJEC shall comprise representative members of all the local education authorities in Wales, together with representatives of teachers in schools and colleges, the University of Wales, the chief education officers and industrial interests in Wales. The WJEC serves as an association of Welsh LEAs, the Regional Advisory Council for further education in Wales and as an examining body for public examinations in schools and in institutions of further education. The Principality thus already has a form of regional machinery not encountered elsewhere, with a long established experience of planning and operating on a regional basis which would no doubt be of value in helping it to respond to new initiatives of the kind we are now proposing.

11.3. The Government have proposed in the Wales Bill to devolve responsibility for non-university higher and further education in the Principality to the Welsh Assembly, and have announced their intention meanwhile to transfer Ministerial responsibility for these matters from the Secretary of State for Education and Science to the Secretary of State for Wales, with effect from 1 April 1978 or as soon as possible thereafter. The transfer of functions which is planned to take place in 1978 will be an internal rearrangement of the way in which the Government conducts its business. The Government have made clear that the two education departments will maintain a concerted approach to matters of common concern to both countries, including the management of higher education. The transfer will entail no change in the present arrangements under which local authorities in Wales are financed, and they will continue to participate, as at present, in joint local authority/central government discussions of public expenditure and educational matters generally. The relations of local education authorities and their institutions with central government will not be substantially affected by the decentralisation. There does not seem to be any reasons of principle why the arrangements we propose should not apply to Wales during the pre-devolution period with the Secretary of State for Wales and the Welsh Office sharing with the Secretary of State for Education and Science and her Department the functions outlined for central government. In practice, the question will need to be considered further in relation to the timing of devolution.

11.4. Looking beyond devolution, it will be for the Welsh Assembly, when constituted, to consider what arrangements should be made for the management of higher education in the public sector in Wales. The present arrangements provide for free interchange of students and joint planning of provision between the two countries. We think it would be of advantage if these could be maintained.

CHAPTER XII

Implementation

Legislation

12.1. The present statutory basis for pooling the cost of maintained sector higher education is contained in Schedule 2 to the Local Government Act 1974. It only permits the pooling of the total cost and fresh legislation would be required to authorise the system of partial pooling recommended in this report. Under our proposals individual local authorities would remain responsible for determining the overall level of expenditure in their institutions (except where they have passed to direct control by the National Body). The National Body, for its part, would negotiate and agree with each local authority the level of its contribution for which it would use funds provided collectively by local authorities through a modified pool.

12.2. We have not been able to consider fully the legal aspects of such an arrangement. The Department has however advised us that, on the understanding that the proposed arrangements for a modified pool would continue to operate within the Rate Support Grant system, it would not be possible to give the National Body formal executive responsibility for authorising the collection and subsequent allocation of pooled funds by way of adjustments to the payment of the needs element of RSG. As is the case under the present pooling arrangements, that would have to remain the responsibility of the Secretary of State. The legislation should however require the Secretary of State, in exercising this responsibility, to have regard to the advice of the National Body, so effectively safeguarding its responsibility. We believe that this would be a satisfactory solution, and we note, in passing, that it would simplify the operation of the reserve procedure recommended in paragraph 6.8 above.

12.3. We recommend that the Department of Education and Science consult further with the other Departments concerned and the local authority associations about the extent of the legislation which may be necessary on this and other matters.

12.4. The Government are in any case committed to wide ranging consultations on our recommendations. It seems unlikely that this process could be completed in time for legislation to be enacted in the present Parliament. We are, however, anxious to see an early start on the implementation of our recommendations.

12.5. In particular, we hope that ways and means can be found as soon as possible to take further some of the matters which we have recommended need further consideration:

    (a) the basis on which contributions to the higher education pool are assessed (paragraph 5.37);

    (b) the extent to which governing bodies can be given greater authority in establishment matters (paragraph 8.10);

(c) the preparation of model financial regulations for adoption by LEAs (paragraph 8.16);

(d) the preparation of advice on articles of government (paragraph 8.29).

12.6. The establishment of new regional advisory councils as recommended in Chapter IX is in our view a matter of some urgency and it may be desirable to take the necessary steps in advance of decisions on our other recommendations.

12.7. Finally, we recommend that as soon as the Government is in a position, following the consultation process, to take decisions on our recommendations as a whole, they should in the light of the prospective parliamentary timetable consider whether the National Body we recommend should be established on a shadow basis to undertake preparatory work pending the enactment of legislation.

CHAPTER XIII

Conclusions and Summary of Recommendations

13.1. In previous chapters we have dealt with various facets of the matters we were commissioned to examine. Before summarising our recommendations it may be helpful if we add some comments to help them to be seen as an articulated whole and mention one or two matters which have an important bearing on our remit.

13.2. Education has been described as a national service locally administered. Its national character is nowhere more marked than in higher education. This is reflected in our recommendation for a National Body charged with advising on the total resources to be made available for maintained higher education and responsible for effectively determining the allocation of national funds between authorities and institutions. It should be seen as a body exercising considerable authority.

13.3. At the same time, our recommendations reflect our desire to see a large measure of responsibility and initiative at local level. There are therefore important limits to the powers of the National Body. It could neither require nor forbid an institution or authority to make any higher education provision or to incur any particular expenditure. Its influence will derive from its responsibility for allocating the funds which local authorities provide collectively and for overseeing their effective use.

13.4. We regard our recommendation that individual maintaining authorities should directly meet part of the cost of the higher education they provide as an essential corollary to the responsibility they would exercise. It is not merely a financial incentive to prudent management but the counterpart of a degree of freedom from absolute control, a freedom which we think is essential to the welfare of the maintained system.

13.5. Our recommendations as to how management functions at the local level should be discharged reflect this same concern to ensure that management and financial responsibilities are delegated not only to local authorities but also downwards to governing bodies, principals, heads of department and other staff. Our recommendations for the carrying forward of savings are put forward not only as an incentive to prudent management but because we believe that initiative and responsibility at any level can only be fostered if there is some source of funds, however small, within the control of management at that level.

13.6. Our recommendations for new regional advisory councils envisage that they should be financed by their member authorities. This reflects our view that they should not be regarded as regional branches of the National Body but as bodies established by local education authorities in a region to enable them better to discharge their own functions. Their responsibility will be to their parent authorities to whom their advice will normally be directed.

13.7. Throughout our discussions we have kept much in mind the existence of an important direct grant sector of higher education. This has a long history of close working with local education authorities. We wish this to continue and we would regret it if one outcome of our recommendations for better management of the maintained sector were to leave direct grant institutions with a sense of isolation. But it is not within our terms of reference to make recommendations in relation to them, and we have refrained from so doing. We believe, however, that if it were the wish of the providing bodies that they should be either associated with or come within the system of national management we propose there would be a ready response from the maintained side. We hope that the Secretary of State will canvass the possibilities of such steps in the consultations which she has undertaken to make on our report.

13.8. We believe that our recommendations for better management will benefit both the availability and quality of maintained higher education. Our assumption has been that standards will continue to be a matter for academic boards, validating bodies and professional institutions. But we recognise that standards are intimately linked to management and financial decisions. Our proposals for the composition of the National Body reflect our concern with the maintenance of standards. We believe that because of this, and because the councils of validating bodies also include representatives from the local education authority world, there is no need to fear that the actions of the National Body in promoting proper economy will be threatening to educational quality. Where necessary the National Body should stand ready to enter into discussion with validating bodies about standards.

13.9. We have placed much emphasis on the need for higher education to be adaptable to the changes which we expect may be required of it in the period up to the end of the century. The terms and conditions of service of academic and other staff will need to reflect this and we hope that the bodies responsible for negotiating them will keep this in view.

13.10. Finally, we recognise that all of us have as the result of our discussions changed our initial views and come closer to the views expressed by others. We believe that our recommendations represent an important step forward towards more rational and effective management of higher education and as such commend them for implementation at an early date. They are as follows:

General
    (i) Since there will be a continuing substantial local authority role in providing higher education, the system for its management should reflect a partnership between national and local levels.   (3.2, 4.8 and 5.4).

National
    (ii) A National Body should be established with the following terms of reference:

'To collect, analyse and present, where appropriate in conjunction with the Department of Education and Science and the University Grants Committee, information affecting the demand for and supply of higher education in the maintained sector; to advise the Secretary of State and the local authority associations on the total provision which should be made for it; to consider and issue guidance on the programmes and estimates submitted to it by authorities and, where appropriate, institutions; to allocate funds for recurrent expenditure and to advise on the allocation of capital expenditure; and to have general oversight of the development of maintained higher education and its cost-effectiveness. (5.2)

(iii) The National Body should be composed as follows:

Independent Chairman		1
Local Authority Members (to be nominated by the local authority associations)		8–9
Institutional Interests		8
(to be nominated by		
NATFHE	3	
CDP	2	
The Secretary of State	3)	
Others (to be nominated by the Secretary of State)		8–10
		25–28

(6.3)

(iv) The Secretary of State should consult widely in making her nominations, and in the case of the three institutional members for whose nomination she would be responsible should consider names suggested by organisations representing management and staff in maintained institutions providing higher education. There should also be consultations between her and nominating bodies before they take their final decisions. (6.4 and 6.6)

(v) Members should serve in a personal capacity and appointment should be for a fixed period renewable. The Secretary of State and organisations nominating members should also be able to nominate a strictly limited number of other persons to receive papers and to serve as alternates. (6.3 and 6.10)

(vi) The DES should be represented at meetings of the National Body by assessors. (6.3)

(vii) The National Body should employ its own staff. (6.11)

(viii) The position of the local authorities in relation to the National Body should be reflected in a special procedure whereby if the local authority members present were united on an issue but in a minority on the National Body, the matter could be referred at their request to the Secretary of State for decision in consultation with the local authority associations. (6.8–6.9)

56

(ix) The funds under the control of the National Body should be provided by local authorities collectively through a pool. (5.22) They should meet the major part of the cost of providing higher education in the maintained sector. (5.11) Maintaining authorities should, however, be responsible for meeting directly up to 15 per cent of the costs of their higher education provision; this direct local contribution should be introduced at a level of 5 per cent and increased by annual stages up to 15 per cent, subject to review before going beyond 10 per cent. (5.38)

(x) The Pooling Committee should be invited to study alternative formulae for determing contributions to the pool and possible transitional adjustments designed to mitigate difficulties arising from the introduction of local contributions. (5.37)

(xi) The National Body's remit should extend to all forms of maintained higher education and it will have to develop a variety of administrative and financial mechanisms appropriate to varying types of institution and provision. We have considered certain possibilities but the National Body should be free to make the final choice, in consultation with the local authority associations and other interested organisations. (7.2–7.3)

Local

(xii) Individual maintaining authorities should retain overall responsibility for the good management of institutions under their control. (8.1) Subject to this, institutions should be granted the maximum freedom to manage their own affairs. (8.3)

(xiii) The governing body of an institution should provide a clear focus of authority and accountability. (8.5) In particular,

    (a) it should be accorded the greatest practicable degree of operational freedom in matters relating to the appointment of all grades of staff; (8.6)

    (b) it should in general be free to make its own arrangements regarding purchases and contracts; and (8.12)

    (c) its ultimate responsibility to its maintaining authority for all expenditure incurred by the institution should be clearly recognised. (8.20)

(xiv) Provision should be made whereby a governing body which fails to fulfil its responsibilities could be dissolved and arrangements made for the discharge of its functions pending the establishment of a new governing body. (8.13)

(xv) Although the business of the governing body should be entrusted to a clerk reponsible directly to it, the chief education officer of the maintaining authority should have the right to attend and speak at all meetings. (8.5)

(xvi) The constitution and modus operandi of the governing body should ensure

(a) continuity of membership among non-staff members to enable them to acquire an adequate understanding of the institution's work;

(b) the association of members with specific areas of the institution's work, eg through finance committees and joint planning committees with the academic board; and

(c) a reasonable overall balance in membership between representatives of the maintaining authority, representatives of interests within the institution itself and independent members.   (8.21)

(xvii) Rules governing finance should ensure

(a) the provision of funds by the maintaining authority in the form of a closed budget, with supplementation only on the basis of pre-determined rules;

(b) the carry-over by the institution from one financial year to the next of at least part of any savings made through effective management; and

(c) the operation of financial planning and control on the basis of rolling programmes.   (8.14)

(xviii) Clear and detailed financial regulations should be drawn up by maintaining authorities governing their relations with their institutions.   (8.16)

(xix) The academic board should have access to relevant financial information to enable it to assess the financial implications of its decisions on academic matters; conversely, the governing body should take into account the advice of the academic board regarding the academic implications of financial decisions.   (8.24)

(xx) The principal as chairman of the academic board should have a major responsibility for ensuring harmonious relations between the latter and the governing body.   (8.25)

(xxi) Those responsible for day-to-day management of the institution should be adequately represented on its governing body and academic board.   (8.26)

(xxii) Responsibility for the formulation of guidance on articles of government and for their approval should remain with the Secretary of State, who should, however, look to the National Body for advice.   (8.29)

(xxiii) The National Body should have a general responsibility for improving the management of maintained higher education as a whole. In addition to preparing advice on articles of government, it should promote further consideration of

(a) the extent to which governing bodies can be given greater authority in establishment matters, and

(b) the preparation of model financial regulations for adoption by LEAs.   (8.10, 8.16 and 8.30)

(xxiv) Further consideration should be given in the appropriate quarters to the responsibility of governing bodies for approving student union fees and to the provisions of the Burnham FE Document affecting the management structure of institutions. (8.17)

Regional

(xxv) Nine new regional advisory councils should be established in England, with responsibility for considering, promoting, monitoring and advising on the planning, coordination and development in the regions of higher education in the public sector, including initial, induction and in-service training of teachers. Universities in each region should be invited to cooperate with these new councils and to be represented on them. (9.12–9.13)

(xxvi) The councils should be set up by trust deeds, requiring the establishment of a governing body, together with two main sub-committees to deal with

(a) higher education, including initial teacher education, and

(b) the induction and in-service training of teachers. (9.16)

(xxvii) Initially, the boundaries of each region should be those of the existing RACs; modifications of these boundaries, where necessary, and arrangements for membership in areas of overlap should be the subject of negotiation between the councils as soon as they are established. (9.14)

(xxviii) Each council should have a governing body composed of three broad groups, comprising

(a) representatives of local education authorities and voluntary providing bodies;

(b) representatives of staff and management in the institutions, and

(c) others, including representatives of commerce and industry, schools and the universities. (9.15)

(xxix) Members of Her Majesty's Inspectorate should attend meetings of the councils as assessors. (9.15)

(xxx) The constitution of the governing body of each council should be subject to the approval of the Secretary of State. (9.15)

(xxxi) The budget of each council should be met from the funds of the constituent local authorities. (9.17)

Wales

(xxxii) The application of the recommendations in this report to Wales should be considered further in relation to the timing of devolution. (11.3)

Implementation

(xxxiii) The DES should consult further with the other Departments concerned and with the local authority associations about the legislation which may be required to implement these recommendations. (12.3)

(xxxiv) Consideration should be given, in the light of the prospective parliamentary timetable, to the establishment of the National Body on a shadow basis to undertake preparatory work pending the enactment of legislation.   (12.7)

(xxxv) There should be an early start on the implementation of our recommendations. (12.4)   In particular, steps should be taken urgently, if necessary before final decisions are taken on the other recommendations, to establish the new regional advisory councils (recommendation (xxv)) (12.6) and to initiate the discussions referred to in recommendations (xi) and (xxiii) (12.5). The DES should assume responsibility for the last, pending establishment of the National Body.   (8.30)

APPENDIX A

List of Organisations and Individuals Submitting Written Evidence to the Working Group

Association of College Registrars and Administrators
Association of Polytechnic Teachers
Association of Principals of Colleges
Chartered Institute of Public Finance and Accountancy
Conference of Principals and Directors of Colleges of Higher Education
Council of Polytechnic Librarians
Governing Body of North-East London Polytechnic
Library Association
National Association of Teachers in Further and Higher Education
National Union of Students
Nottingham Professional Committee for Teacher Education and Training
Science and Education Sub-Committee of Labour Party NEC
Standing Academic Planning Board, City of Bradford Metropolitan Council
Standing Conference of Heads of Mechanical and Production Engineering in the Polytechnics
Standing Conference of Regional Advisory Councils
Professor K Alan-Smith and Dr R Horwitz, London Regional Management Centre
Mr G Hutchinson, Chief Education Officer, London Borough of Enfield
Mr John Pratt, Mr Tony Travers and Mr Tyrell Burgess, Centre for Institutional Studies, North East London Polytechnic
Mr J Rendel Jones, Chief Education Officer, East Sussex County Council
Mr E E Robinson, Principal, Bradford College

APPENDIX B

Table Advanced courses in public sector institutions: expected pattern of institutions 1981 and related student numbers 1975/76 analysed by level of study and mode of attendance (England and Wales)*

Type of Institution	No.	Degree and Postgraduate				HND/HNC				Other			
		FT†	SW†	PTD†	EO†	FT†	SW†	PTD†	EO†	FT†	SW†	PTD†	EO†
Polytechnics	30	39,740	21,130	7,250	3,260	4,640	7,020	11,260	1,530	32,470	2,080	19,430	11,550
Other Institutions:													
i. *with more than 90% advanced work*													
Former Colleges of Education freestanding or amalgamated with other colleges	57	14,990	–	240	420	–	–	30	–	38,590	240	1,900	540
Colleges of Music and Drama	2	30	–	–	–	–	–	–	–	1,020	–	–	–
Colleges of Art and Design	3	1,120	30	–	–	–	–	–	–	–	–	–	–
Direct grant FE colleges not included above	2	710	–	–	–	–	–	–	–	320	–	40	50
Other FE colleges	3	270	–	–	–	–	–	–	–	330	–	20	–
i. Sub-total	67	17,120	–	240	420	–	–	30	–	40,260	240	1,960	590
ii. *with between 30% and 90% advanced work*													
Former Colleges of Education amalgamated with other colleges	18	4,220	200	710	570	860	1,180	4,160	400	12,810	650	4,790	3,350
Colleges of Music and Drama	5	40	–	–	–	–	–	–	–	930	–	–	–
Colleges of Art and Design	14	2,770	30	10	–	–	–	–	–	390	–	30	–
Colleges of Agriculture	5	20	–	–	–	–	780	–	–	50	–	–	–
Direct grant FE colleges not included above	1	–	–	–	–	–	–	–	–	40	–	–	–
Other FE colleges	14	990	90	220	200	1,360	1,080	2,750	600	2,520	310	3,870	2,620
ii. Sub-total	57	8,040	320	940	770	2,220	3,040	6,910	1,000	16,740	960	8,690	5,970
iii. *with less than 30% advanced work*													
Former Colleges of Education amalgamated with other colleges	2	170	–	–	–	–	–	–	–	1,160	–	260	210
Colleges of Art and Design	2	–	–	–	–	–	10	410	100	30	–	–	–
Colleges of Agriculture	5	–	–	–	–	–	120	–	–	20	20	–	–
Other FE colleges	255	90	–	1,040	270	850	1,880	13,040	1,420	4,140	1,310	16,210	10,940
iii. Sub-total	264	260	–	1,040	270	850	2,010	13,450	1,520	5,350	1,330	16,470	11,150
TOTAL	418	65,160	21,450	9,470	4,720	7,710	12,070	31,650	4,050	94,820	4,610	46,550	29,260

* This Table represents the position as forecast in autumn 1976 and takes no account of any further changes which may result from the Secretary of State's announcement on teacher training targets of June 1977.

† FT = Full-time, SW = Sandwich, PTD = Part-time Day, EO = Evening Only.

63

APPENDIX C

The Mechanics of Pooling

1. This Appendix sets out how the existing pooling arrangements operate and how the present arrangements might need to be modified on the introduction of the system of finance envisaged in this report.

2. The present statutory basis of pooling is contained in Schedule 2 to the Local Government Act 1974, and in Regulations (the Rate Support Grant (Adjustment of Needs Element) Regulations 1976) made under that Act. The pooling arrangements work as follows:

(i) Each local education authority submits annually a return of its estimated expenditure on the provision of higher education eligible for pooling as defined in the Regulations. This return constitutes that authority's *claim* on the pool.

(ii) The Department of Education and Science adds these claims together and the resulting national total is then reapportioned amongst all local education authorities on the basis of an agreed general formula to establish each local education authority's *gross contribution* to the pool. Since 1975/76, the apportionment formula has been on the basis of school population (69 per cent of the combined national total) and non-domestic rateable value (31 per cent).

(iii) Each local education authority's gross contribution is subtracted from its claim to produce its *net pool receipt or contribution.* Since pooling is essentially a balancing calculation, nationally the net receipts and contributions add up to zero.

(iv) Finally the Department notifies the Department of the Environment of the net receipts or contributions arrived at for each local education authority to enable appropriate adjustments to be made to the payment of Rate Support Grant (RSG) needs element. The transfer of resources between local education authorities is thus achieved by adjusting each authority's share of RSG needs element upwards or downwards by the amount by which its claim on the pool either exceeds or falls short of its gross contribution to the pool.

3. Under the proposals outlined in this report, the costs of running higher education, hitherto pooled in their entirety, would be met by contributions from the individual maintaining authorities and by pooled funds provided collectively by all local education authorities. Moreover, the total national cost of maintained higher education and, therefore, the total size of the pool would be determined in advance. How this could happen is decribed below:

(i) Each local education authority would submit annually to the National Body a return of its estimated expenditure on the provision of higher education. On the basis of those returns, the National Body would submit its advice to the Secretary of State on the quantum of provision for higher education in the maintained sector. That advice would then form part of the information available to the DES and Welsh Office and the local authority associations in the annual discussions of relevant expenditure eligible for Rate Support Grant. Those discussions take place initially, in respect of Education and related activities, in the Expenditure Steering Group on Education, and are then referred to the Consultative Council on Local Government Finance which covers the whole area of RSG. The quantum available for higher education would be decided in the context of the Rate Support Grant settlement and would be separately identified.

(ii) A proportion of the total national cost so determined would fall to be met directly by individual local education authorities in respect of their own institutions. The proportion met nationally by LEAs in this way would rise from 5 per cent initially to a maximum of 15 per cent, subject to a review at 10 per cent. The balance of the expenditure determined within the Rate Support Grant negotiation would be pooled amongst all local education authorities.

(iii) As at present, the gross contribution to the pool of each local education authority might be determined by the Department on the basis of an agreed national formula. Each authority's claim on the pool would however be determined after negotiations between

65

it and the National Body. The procedures used for this purpose would be for the National Body to decide but some possible mechanisms—per capita payments, payments for individual courses, and finance based on total higher education programmes—are described in Chapter VII.

(iv) Finally, it would be for the National Body to advise the Secretary of State for Education and Science of the allowable claims on the pool for each local education authority constrained by the quantum mentioned in (i) above. On the basis of that information, the Department would notify the Department of the Environment, as at present, of the net receipts or contributions arrived at for each local education authority to enable appropriate adjustments to be made to the payments of RSG needs element. As at present, nationally the net receipts and contributions would add up to zero: our proposals would not entail any increase in the aggregate needs element of RSG.

Produced in England for Her Majesty's Stationery Office by Commercial Colour Press, London E.7
Dd.594851 K16 6/78 CCP